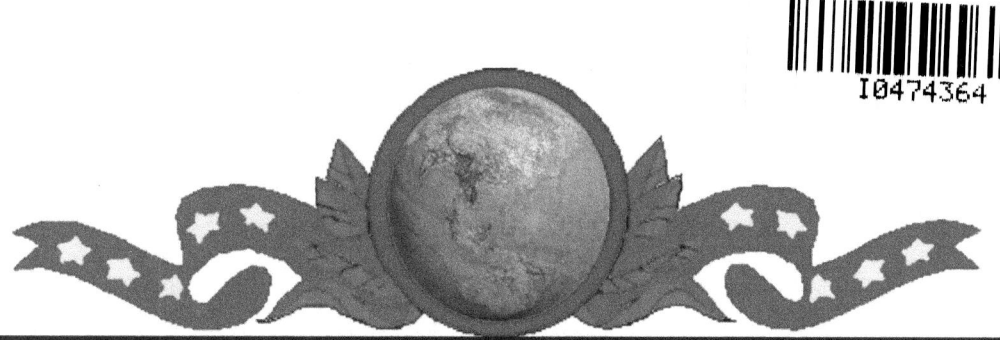

Real World
Colouring Book
For Advanced Users & Adults

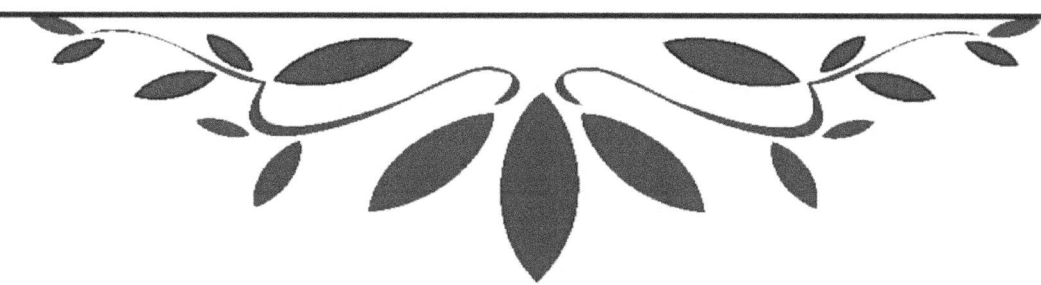

Copyright 2019 Effects By John Boom

50 Images

**Created From Real Life Photos
For You To Colour As You Please.**

ISBN 978-0-359-86491-1
90000
9 780359 864911

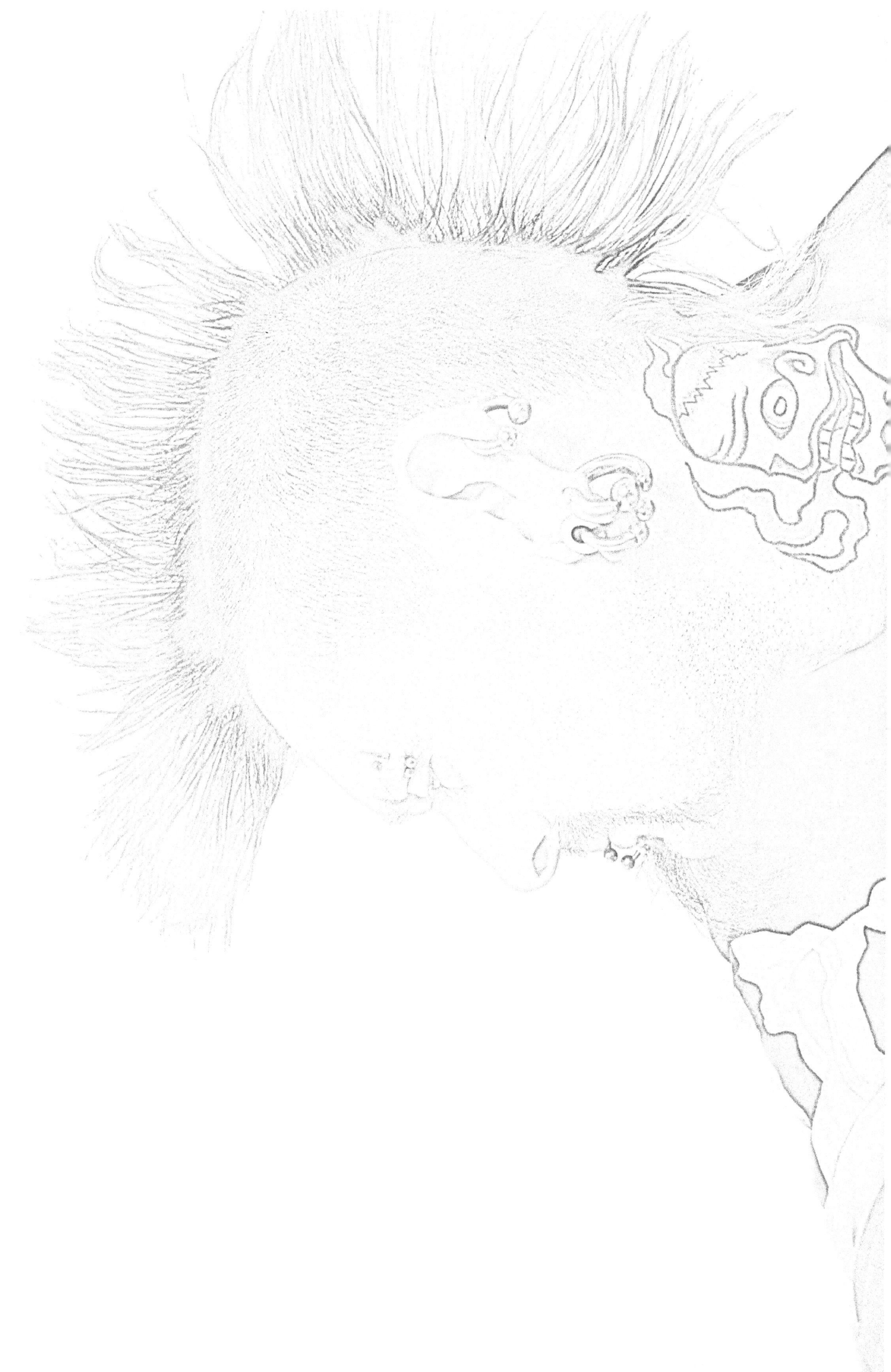

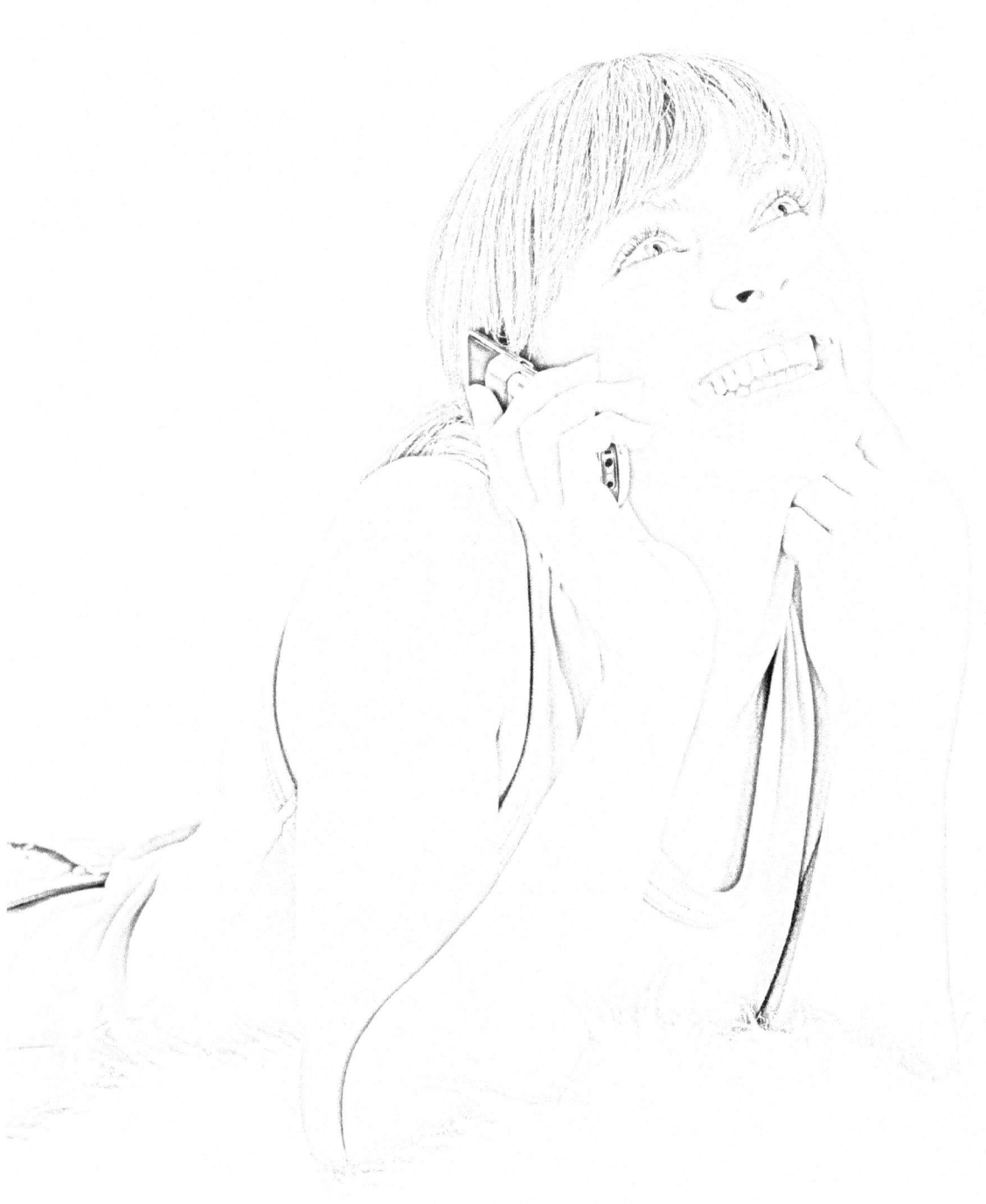

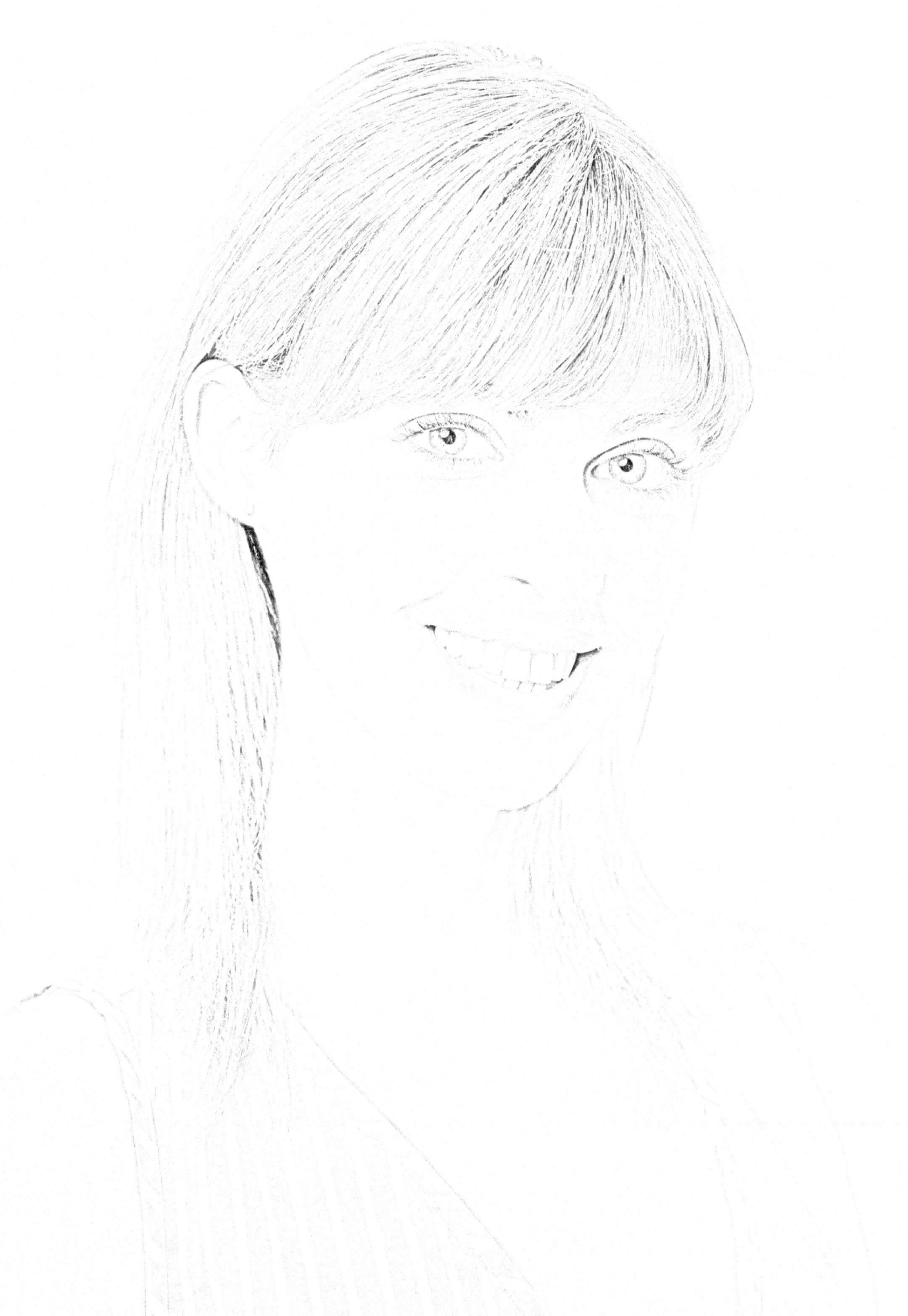

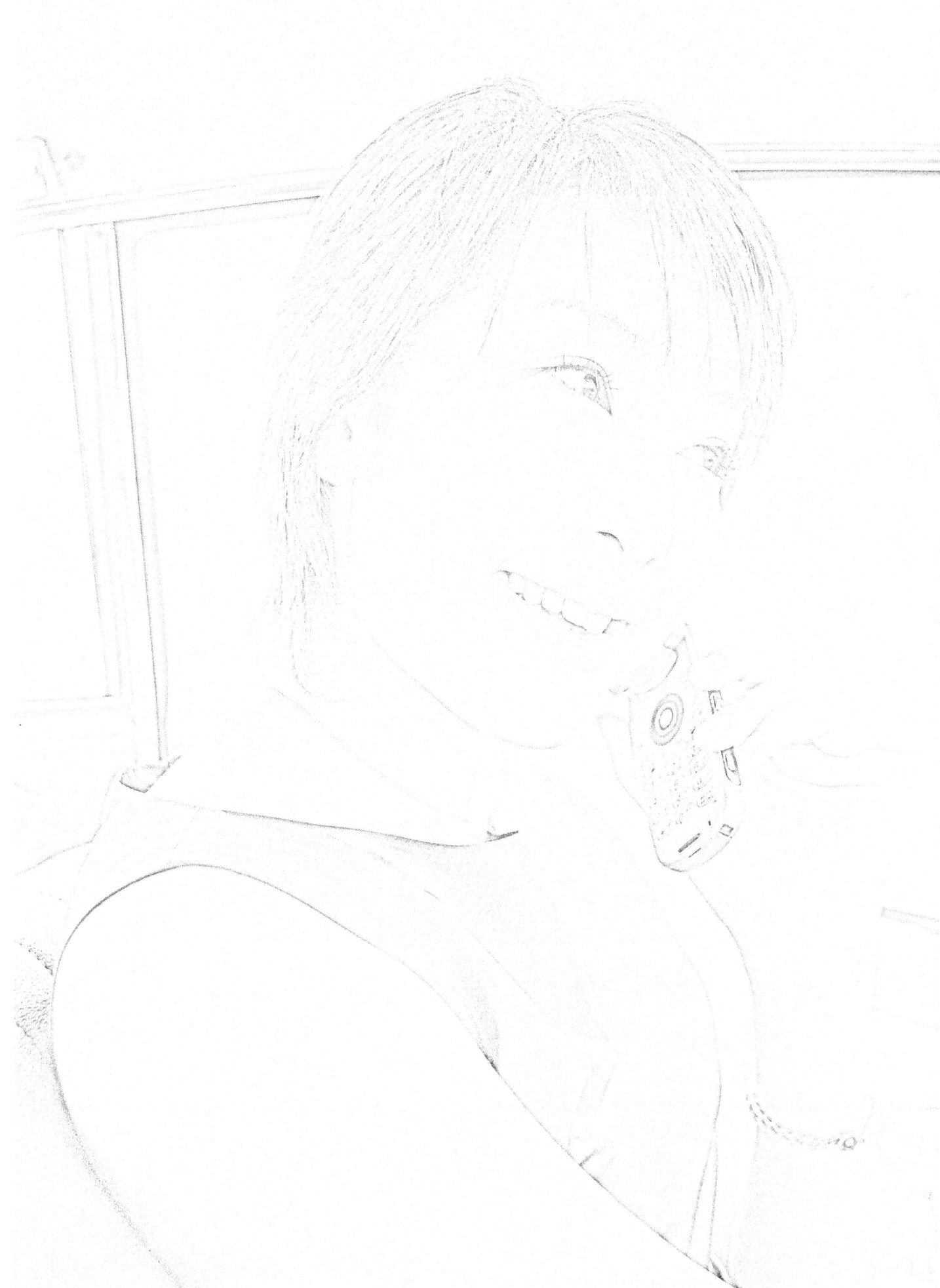

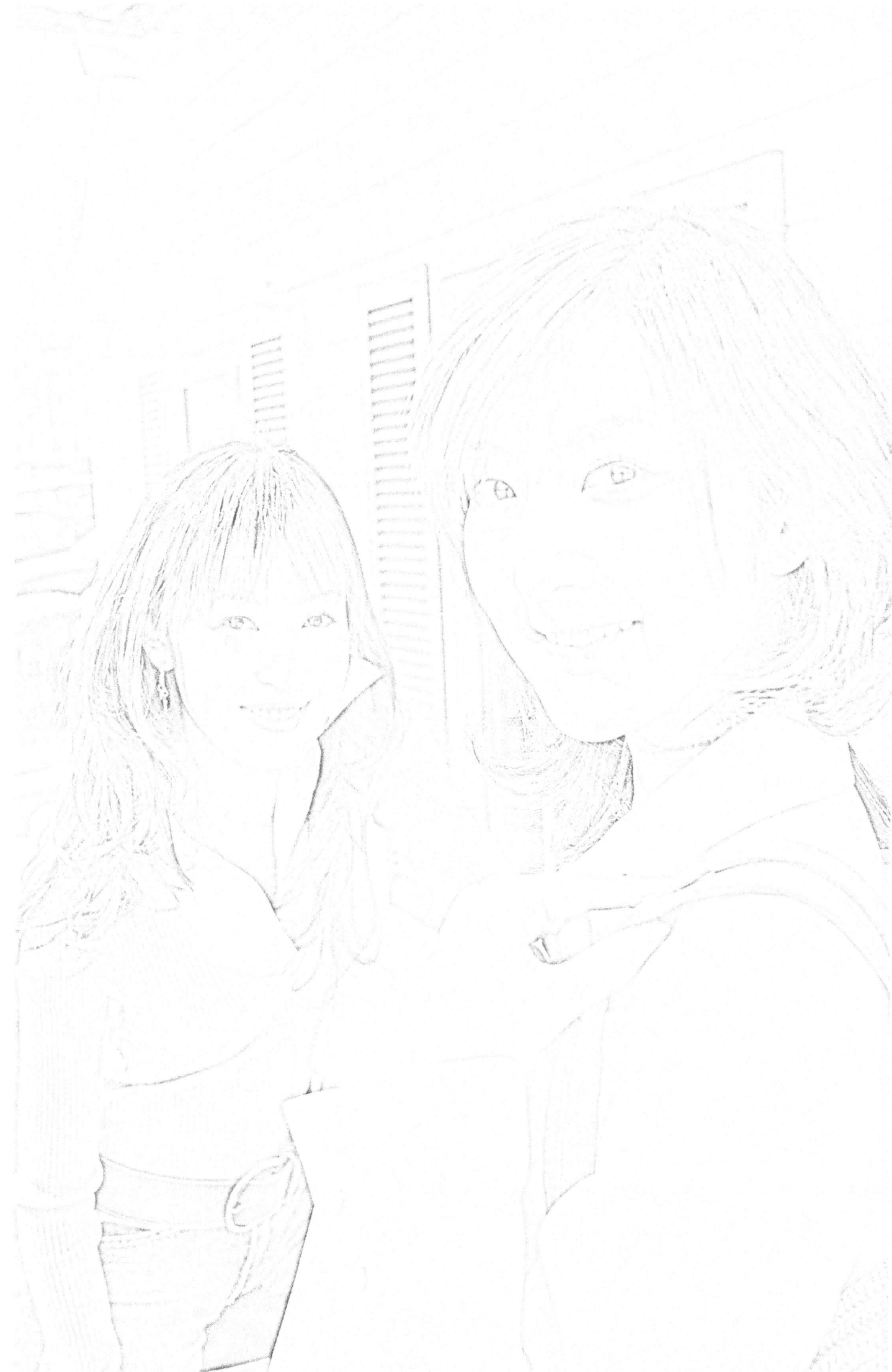

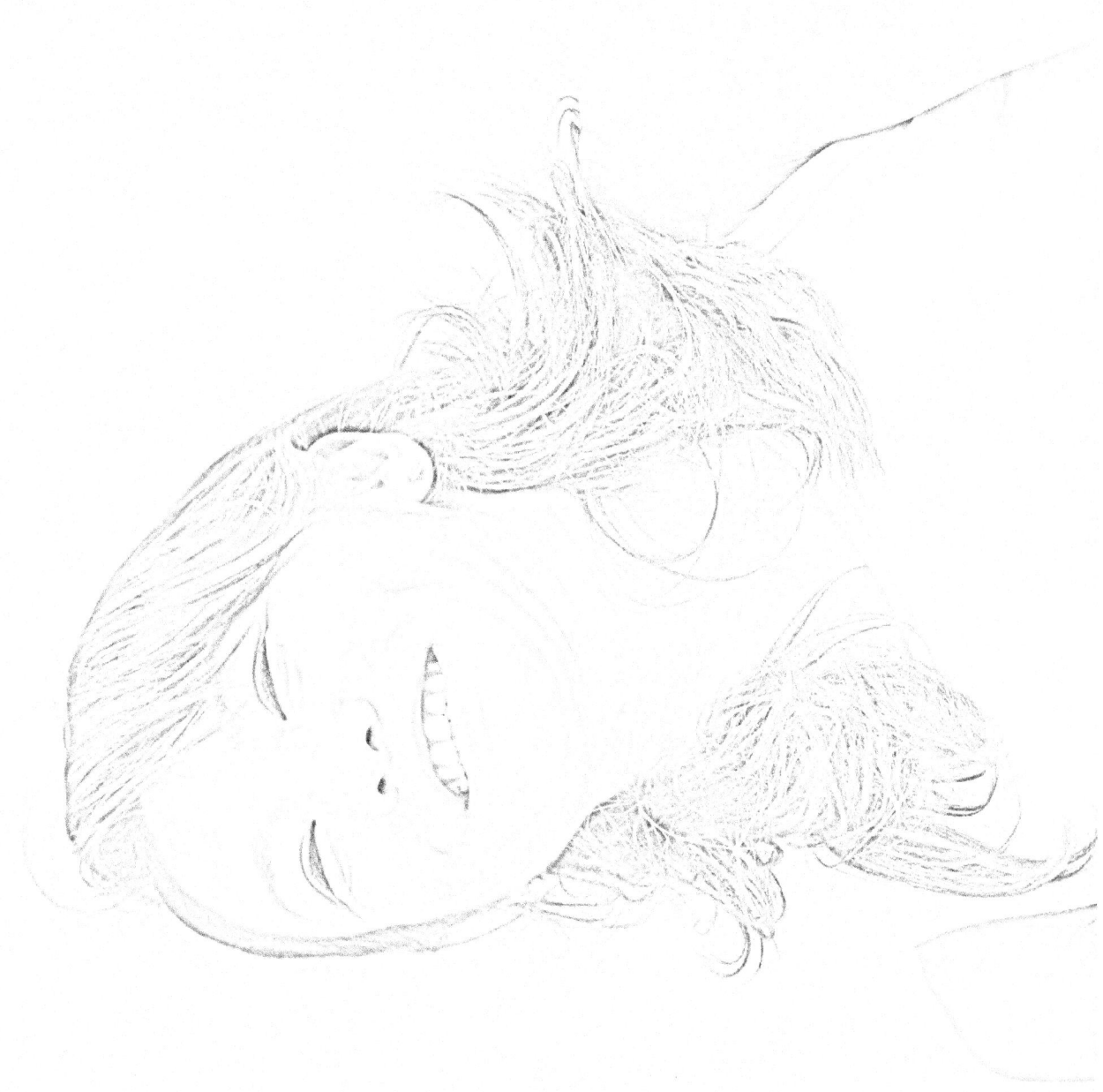

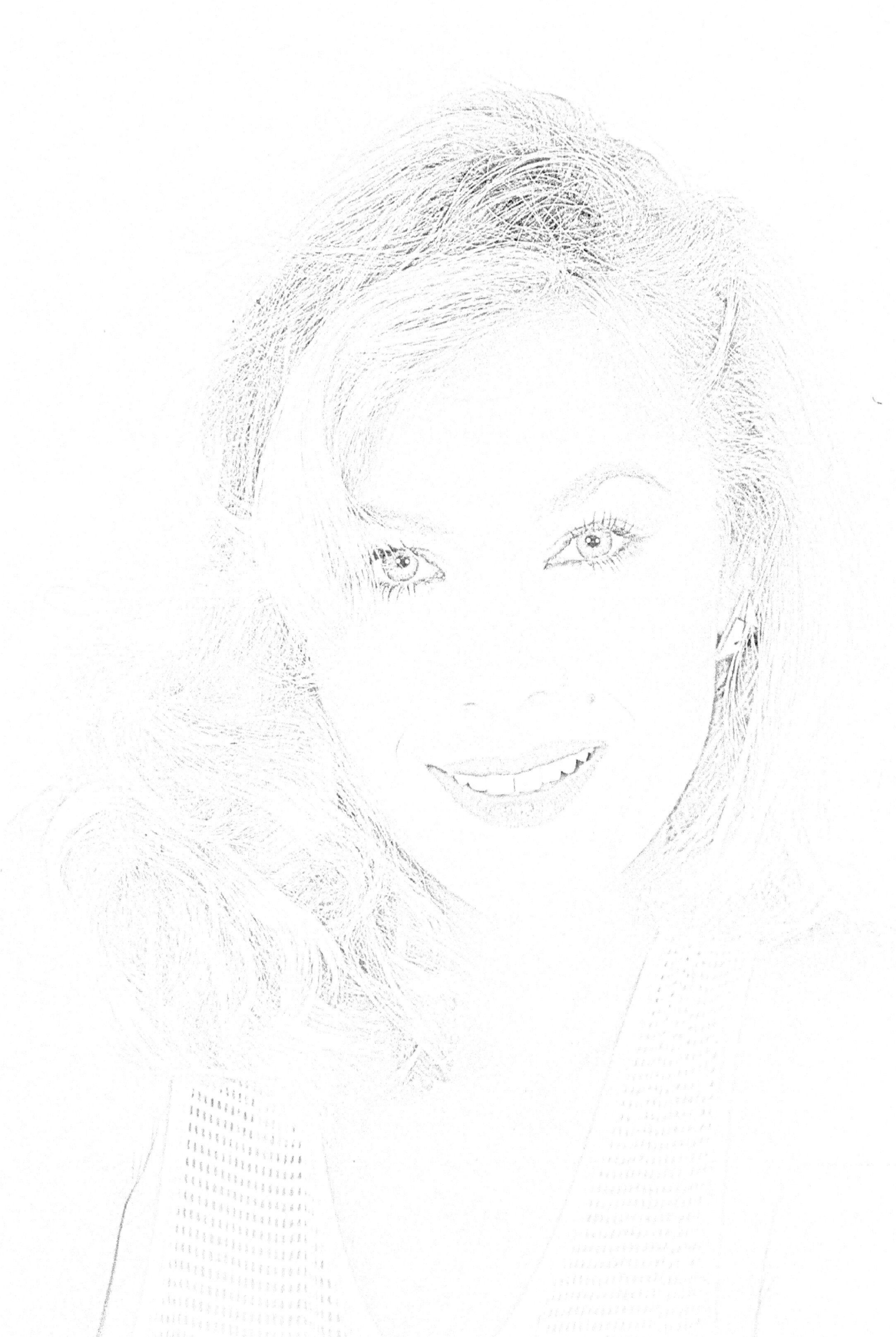

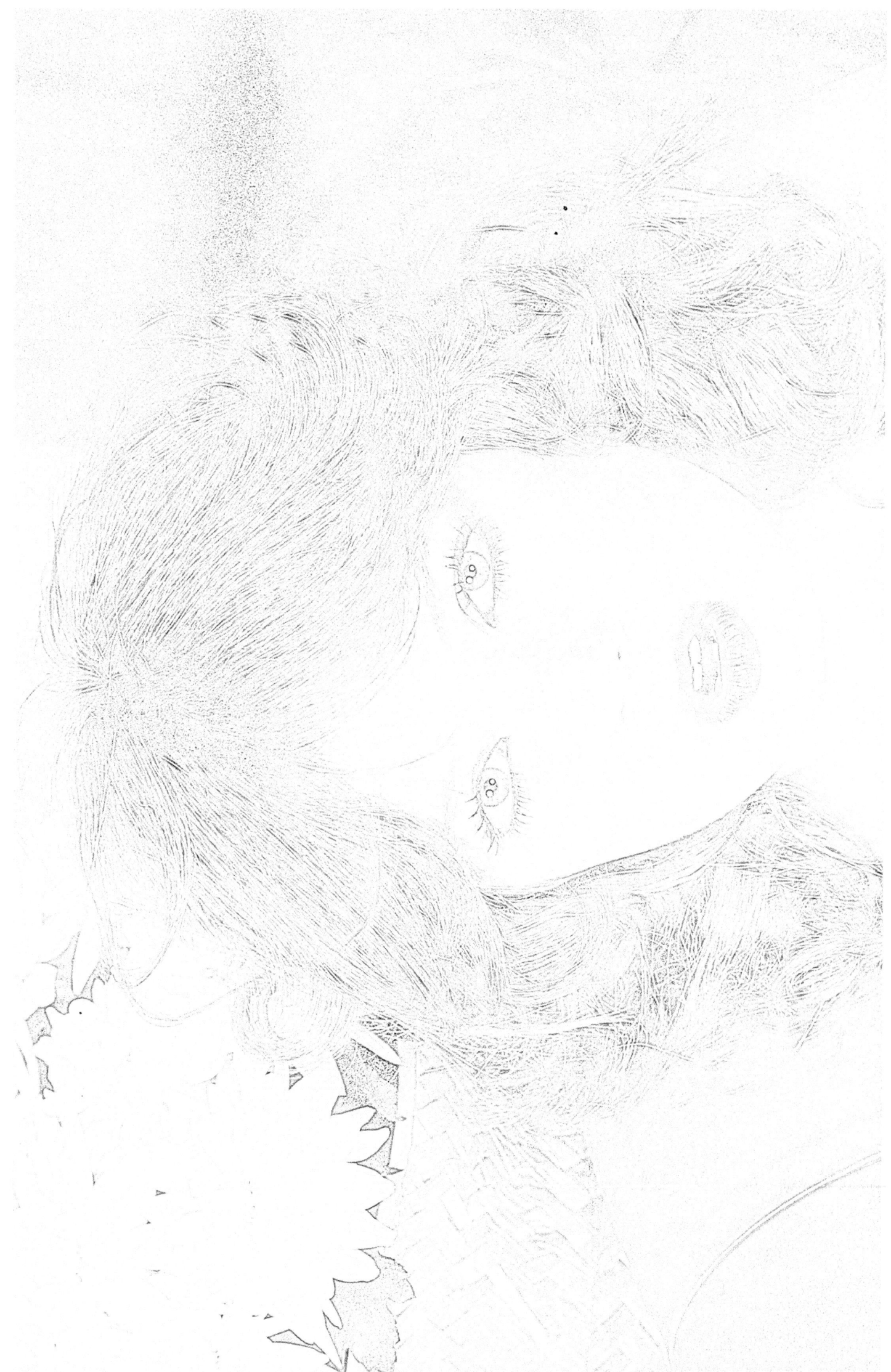

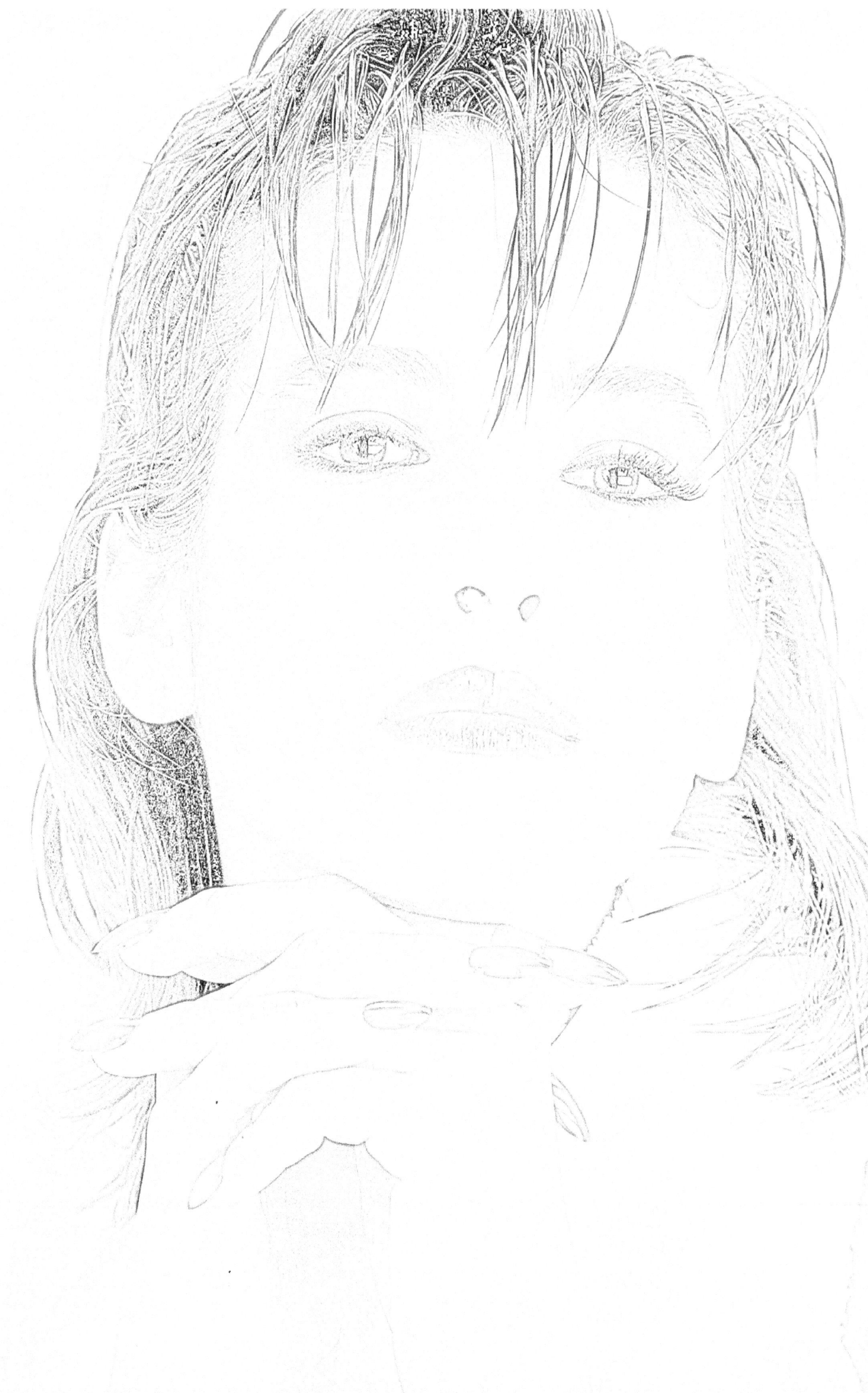

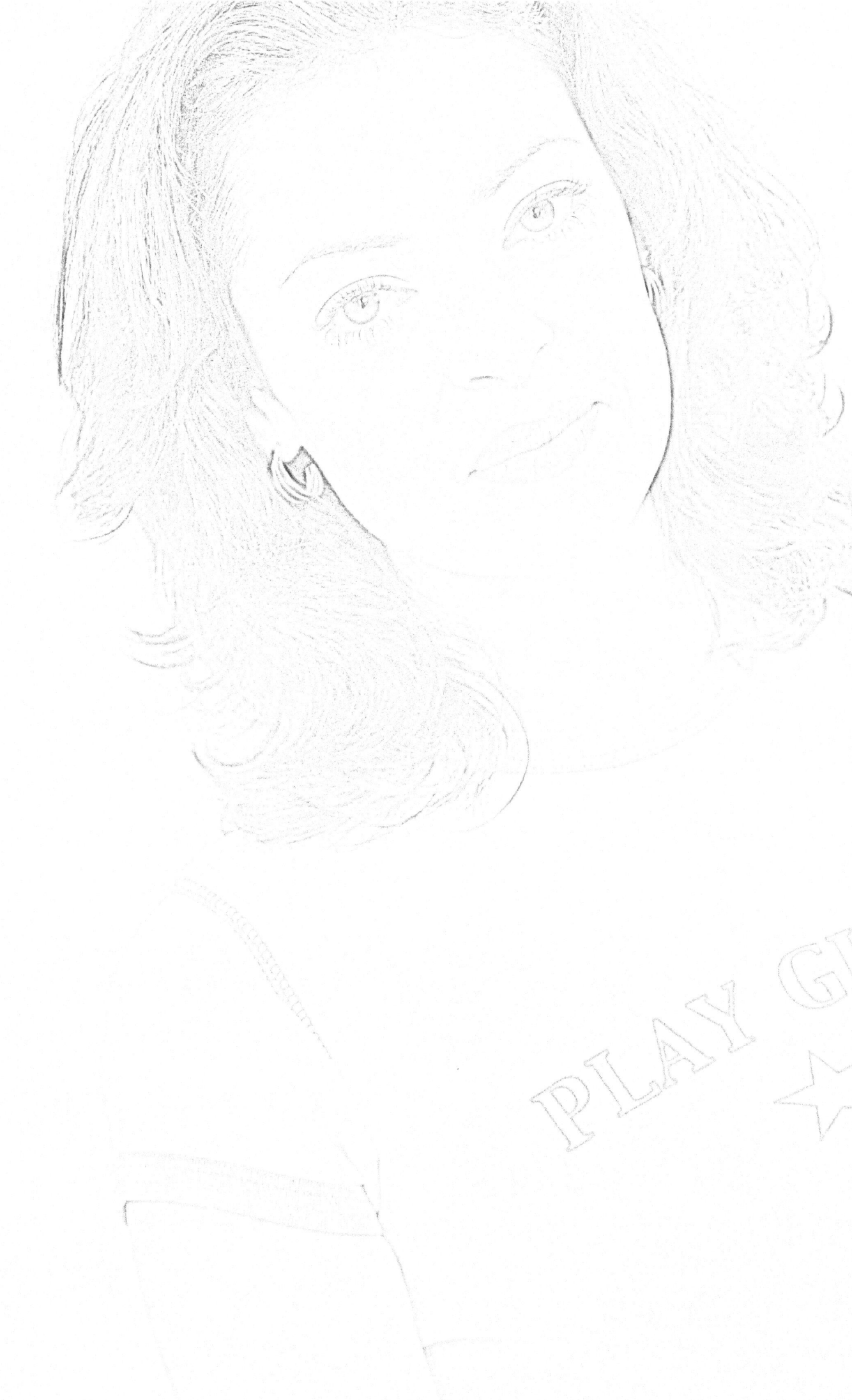

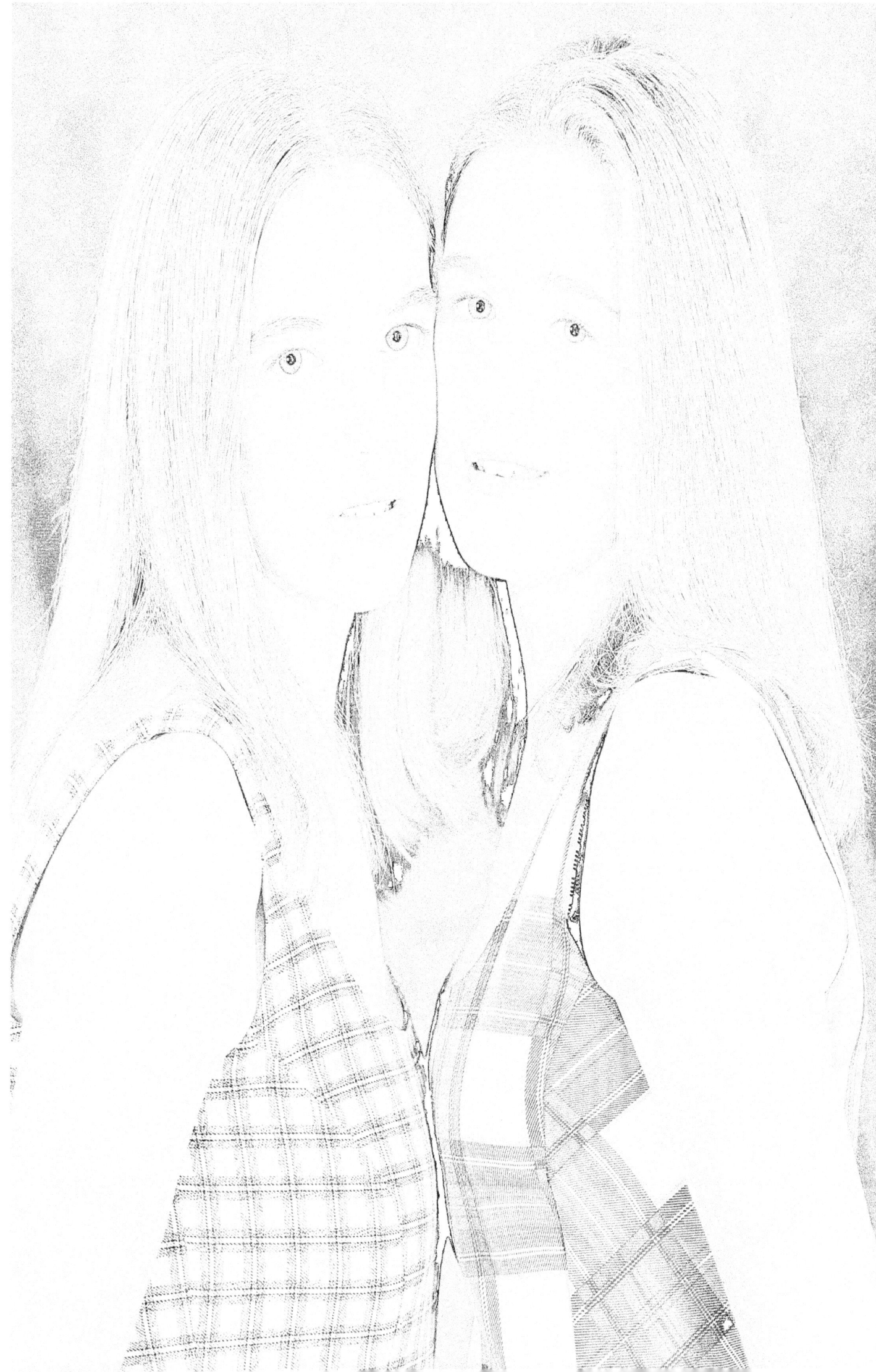

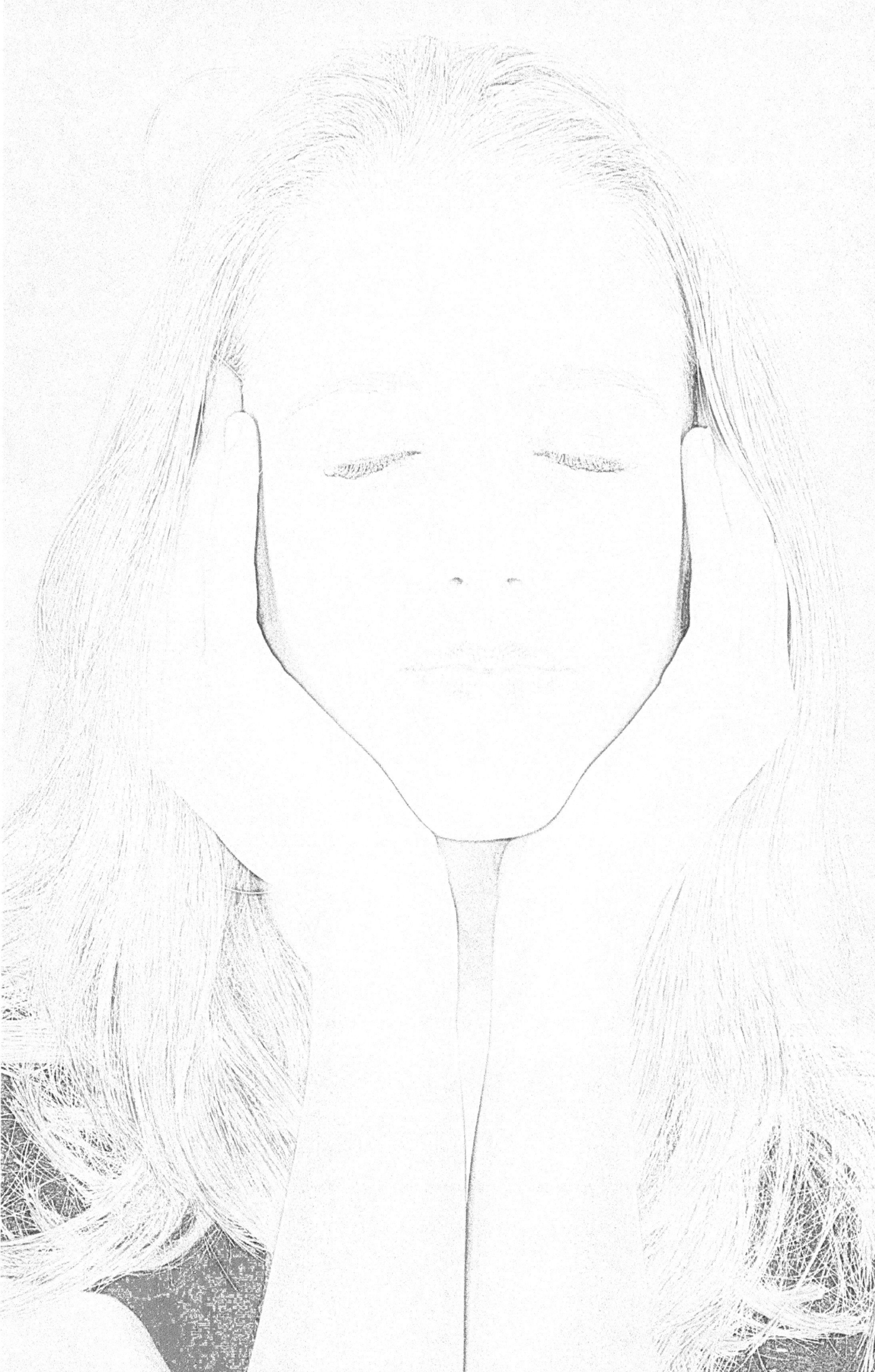

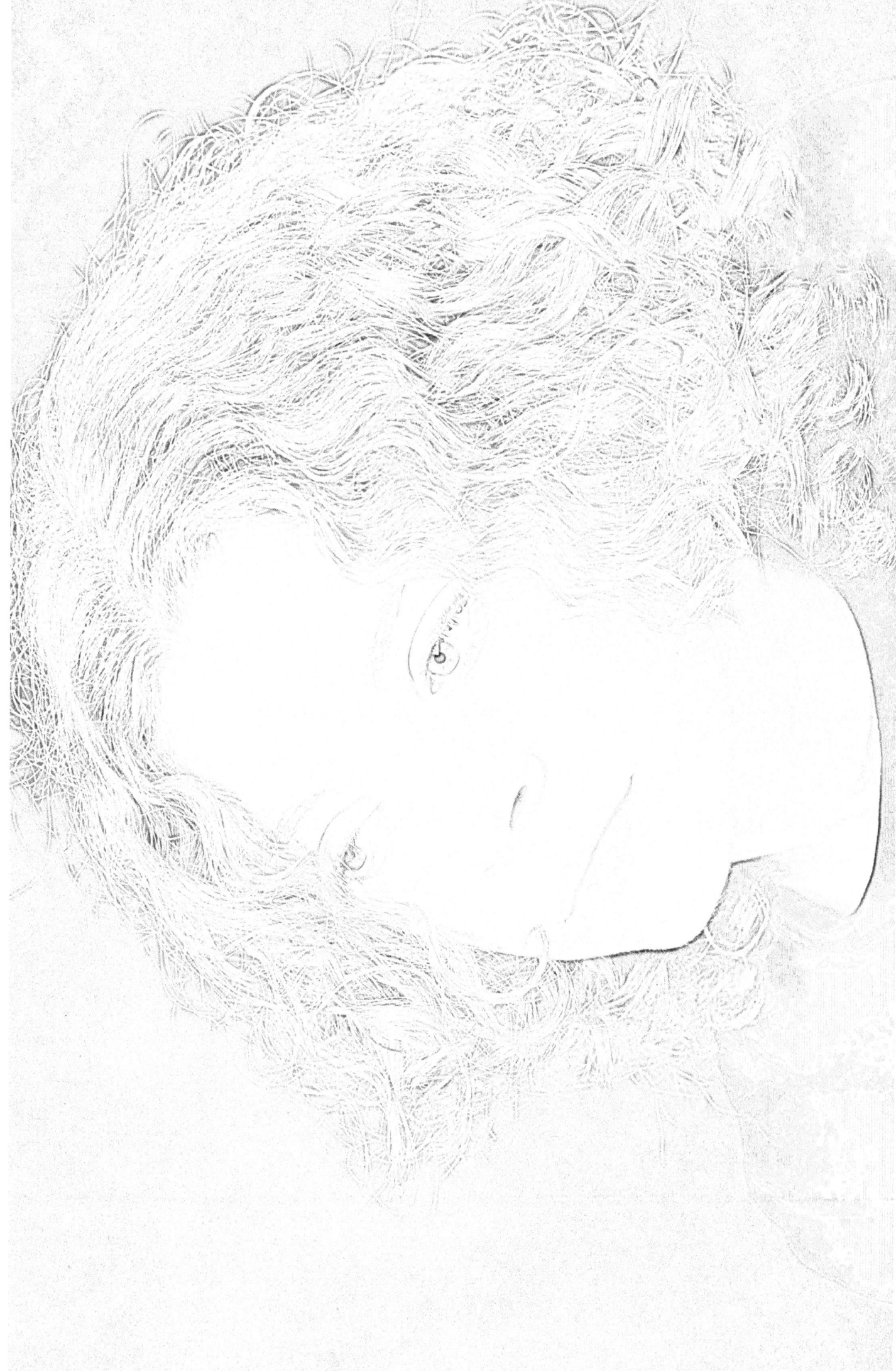

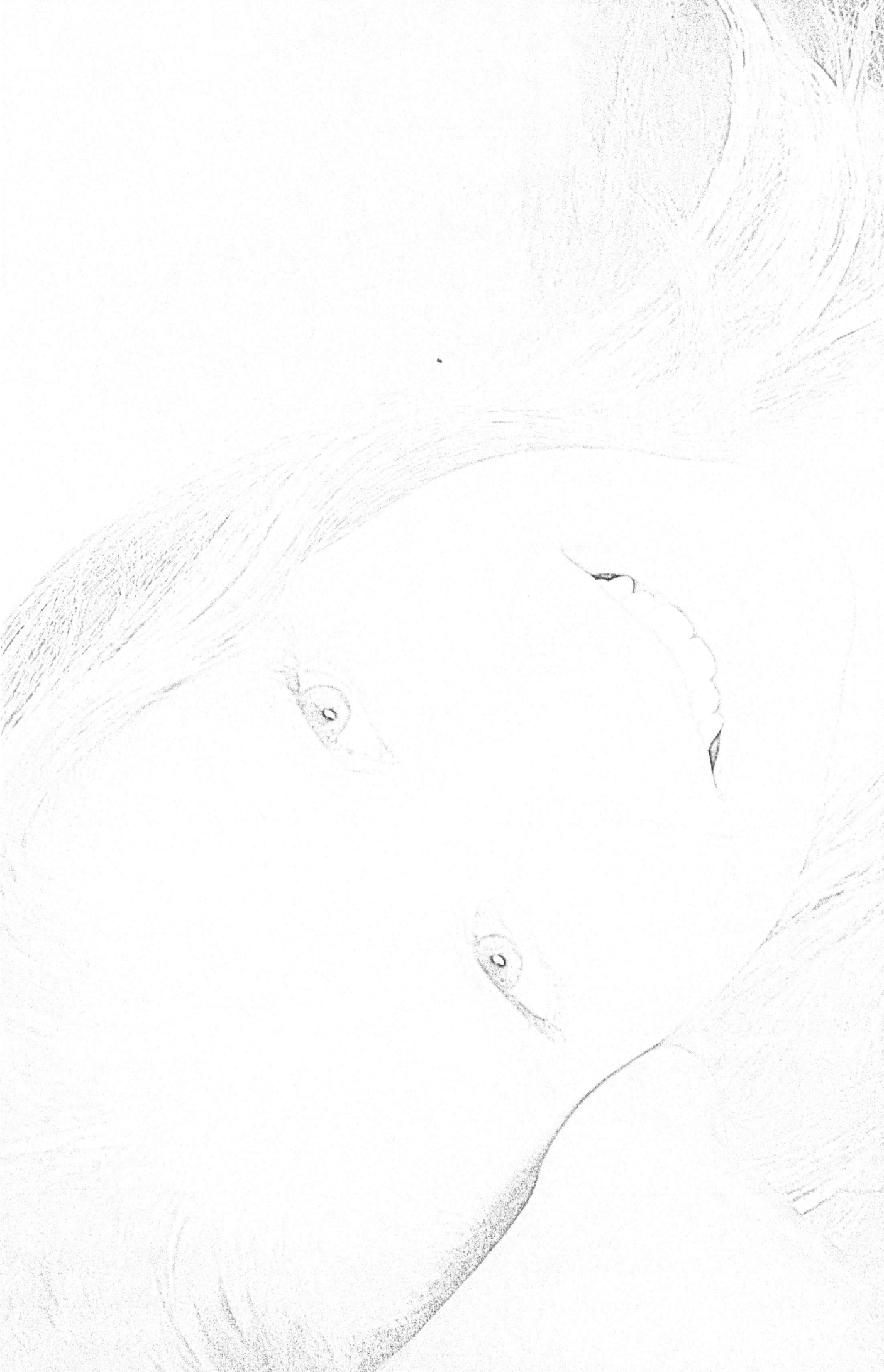

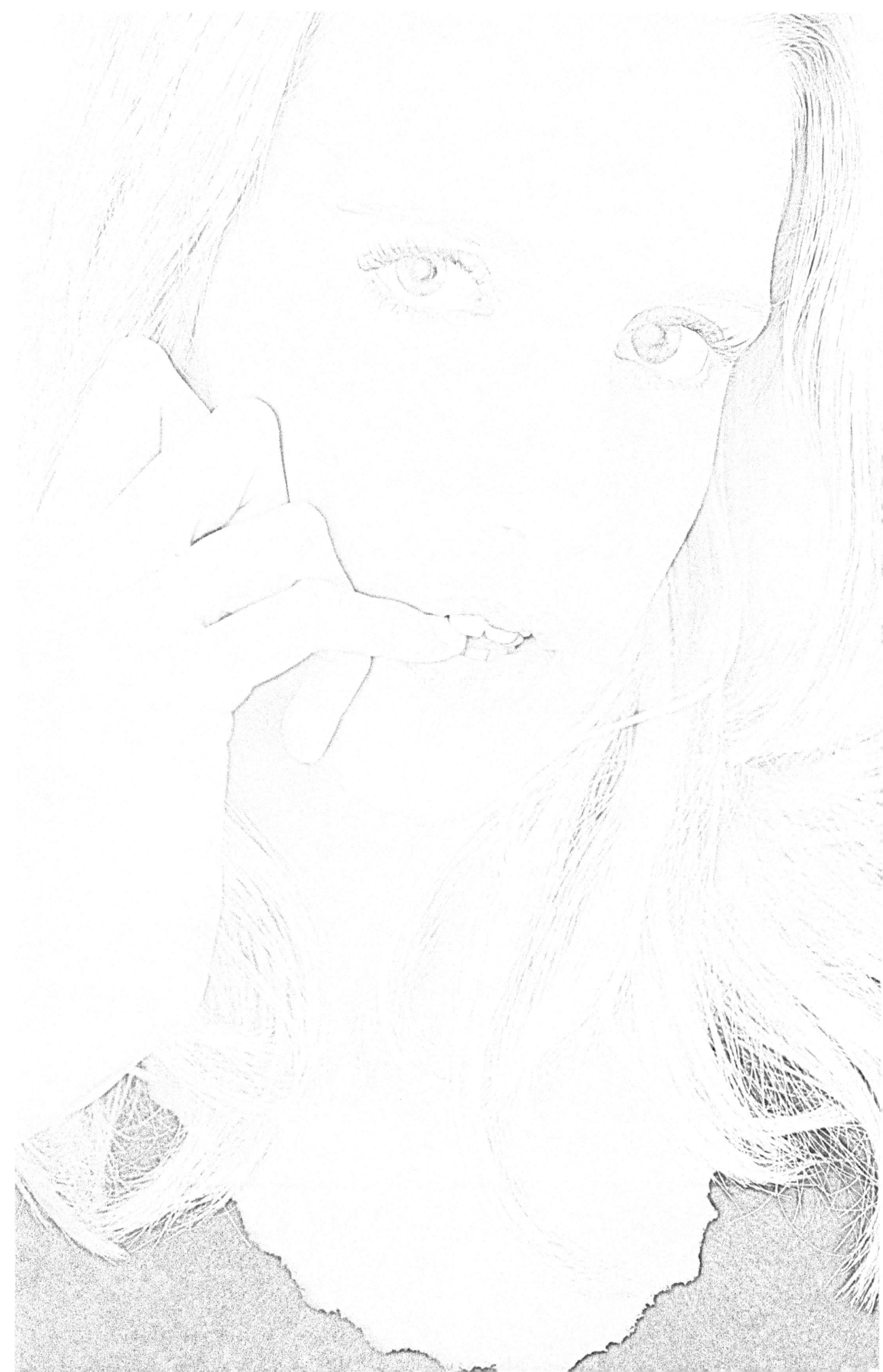

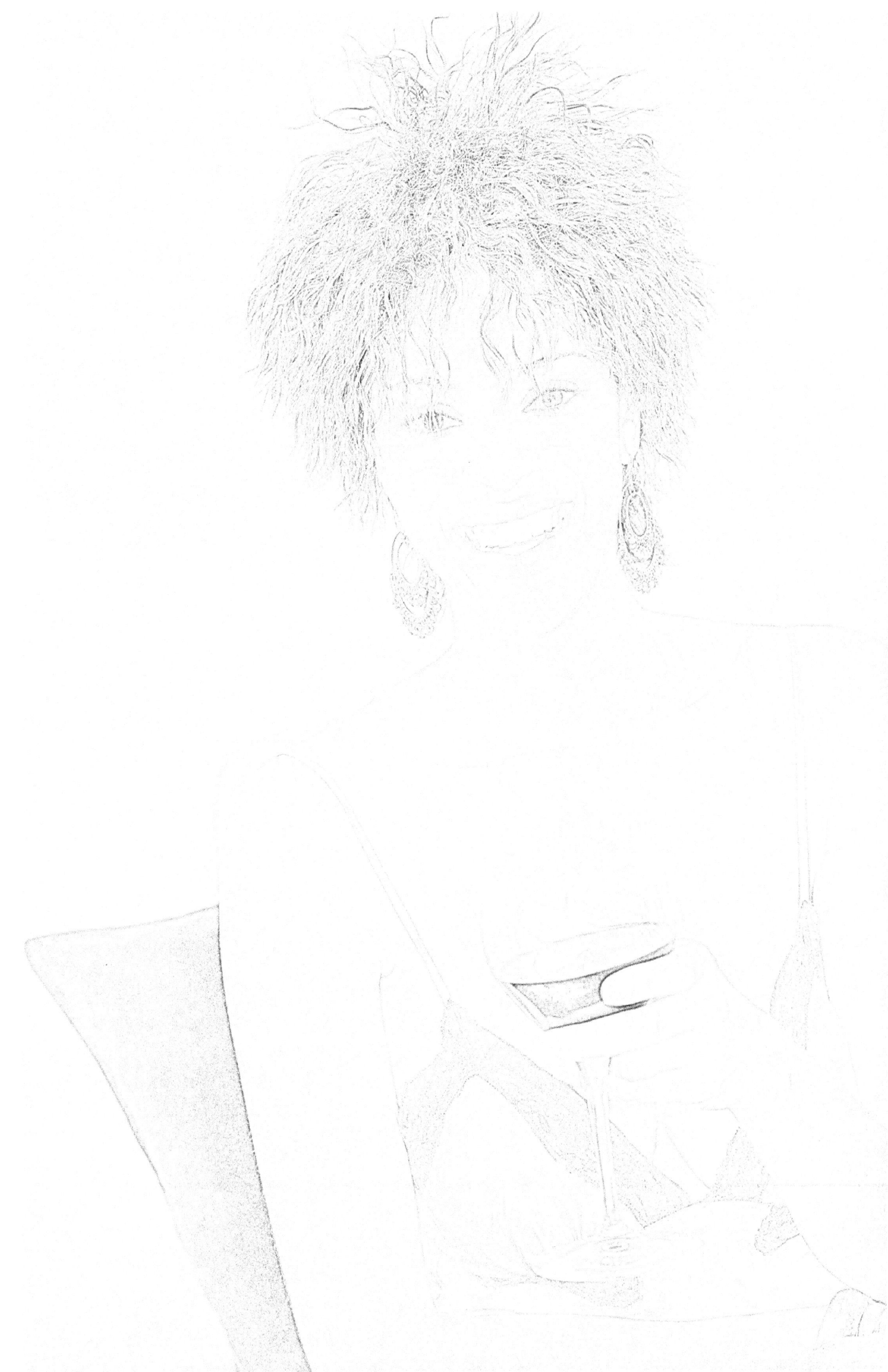

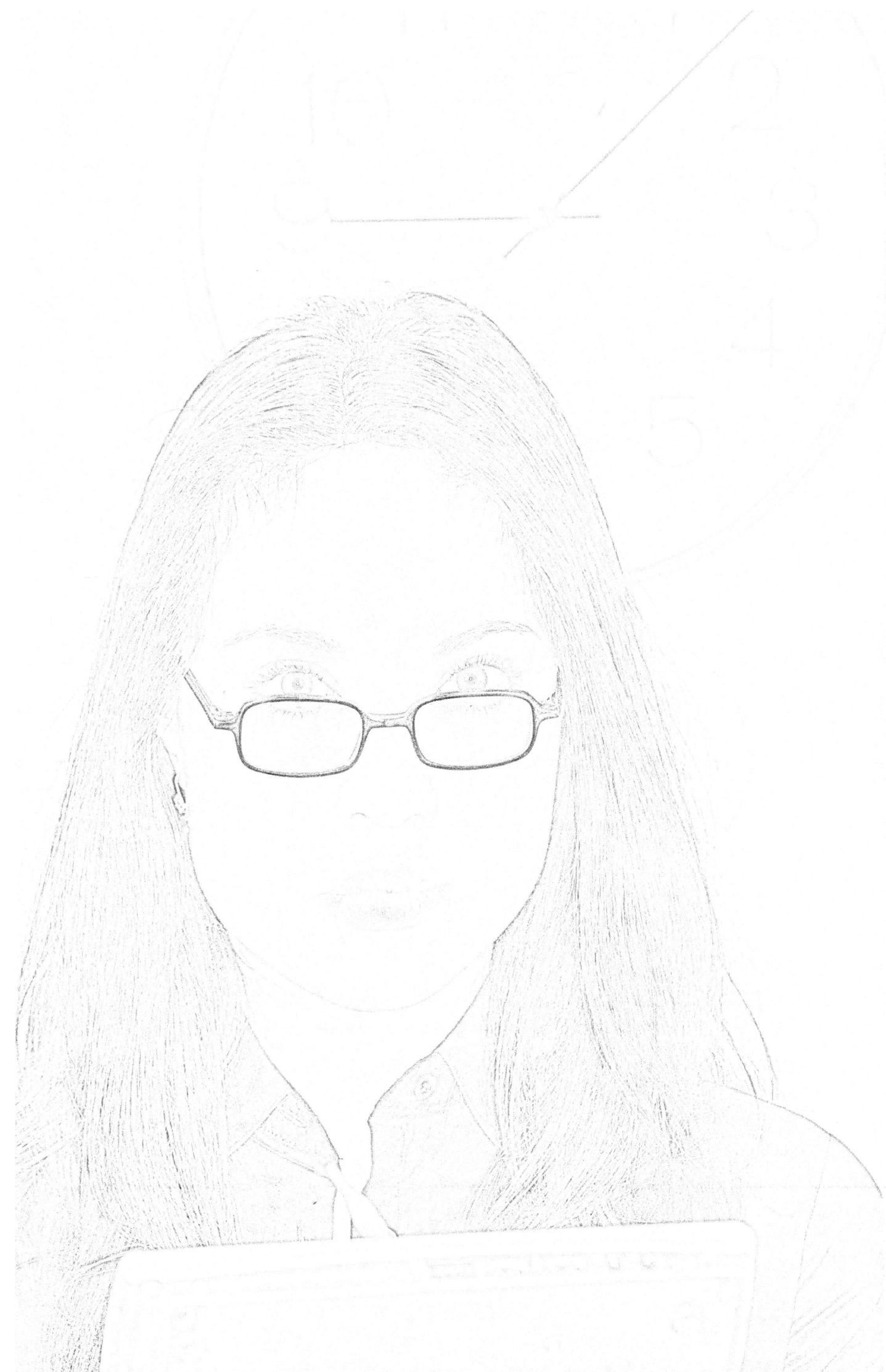

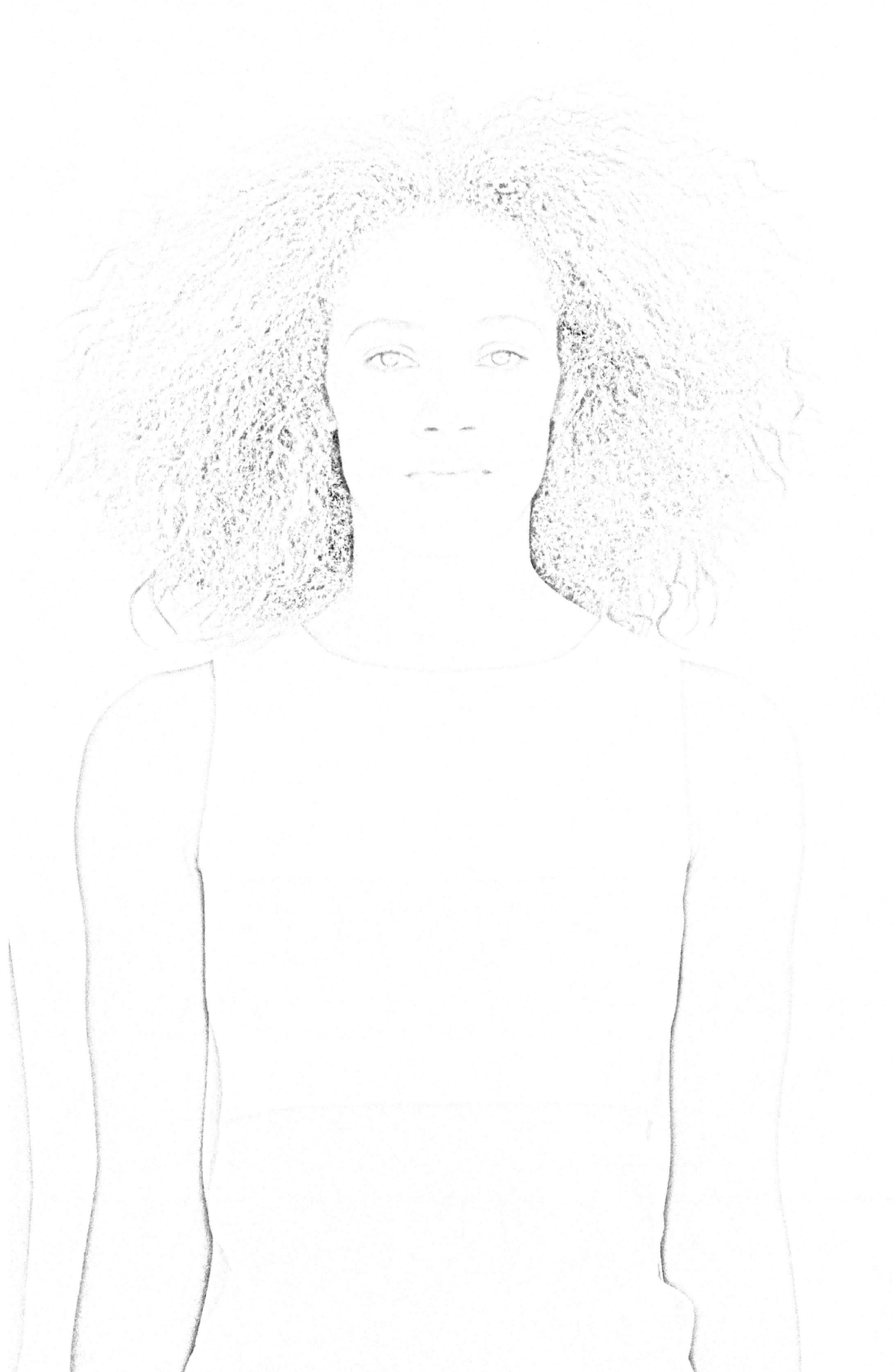

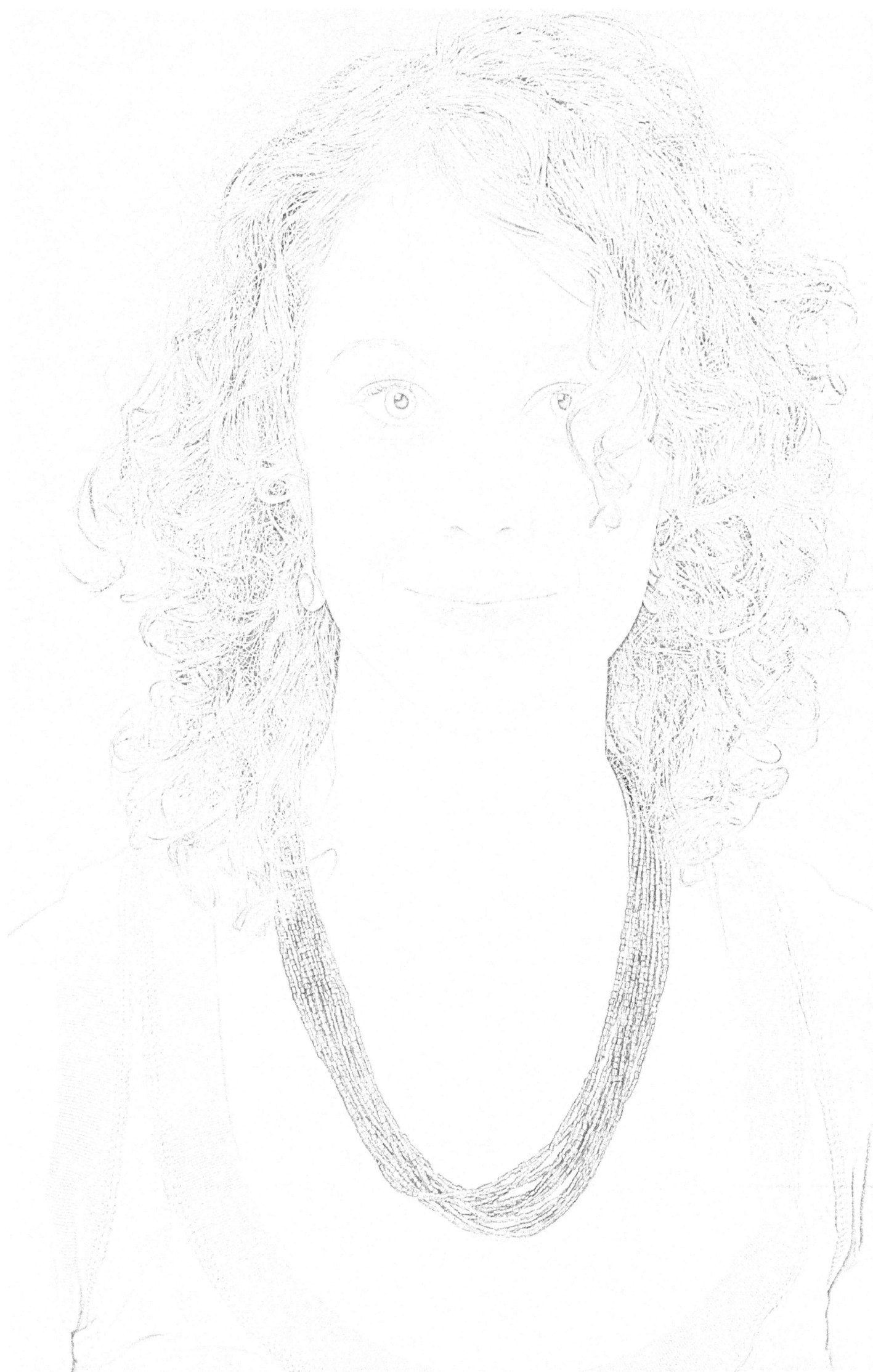

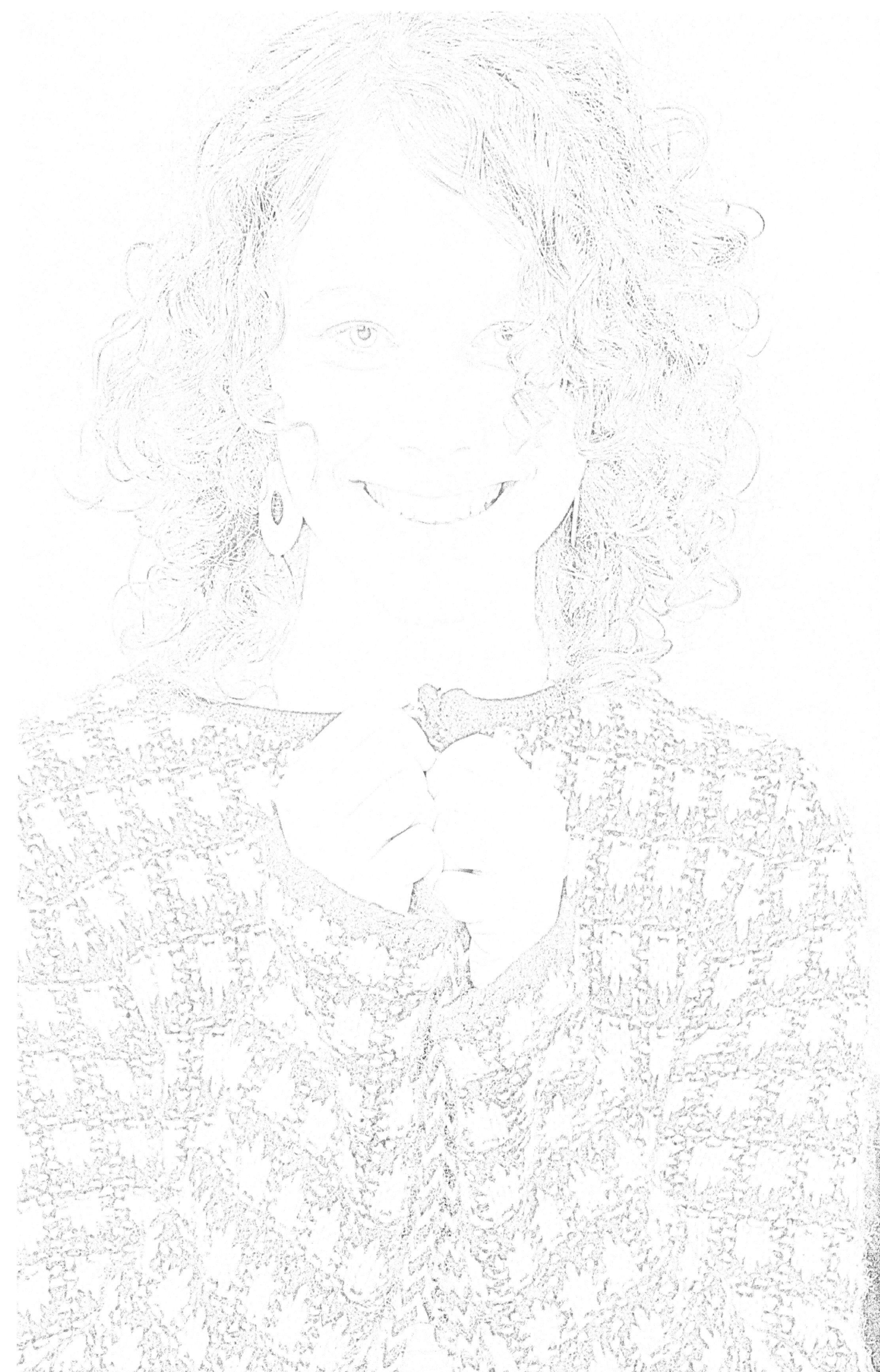

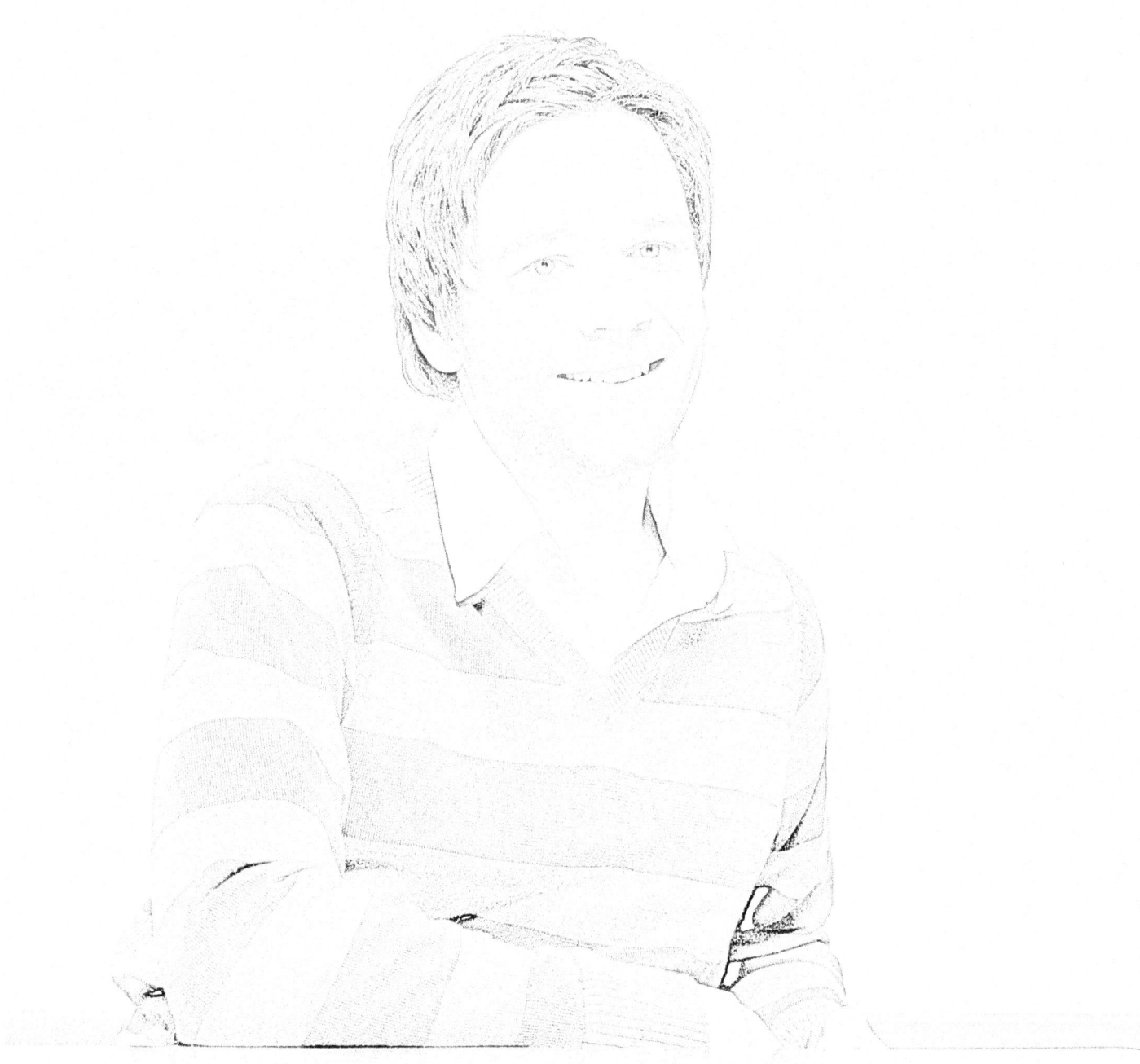

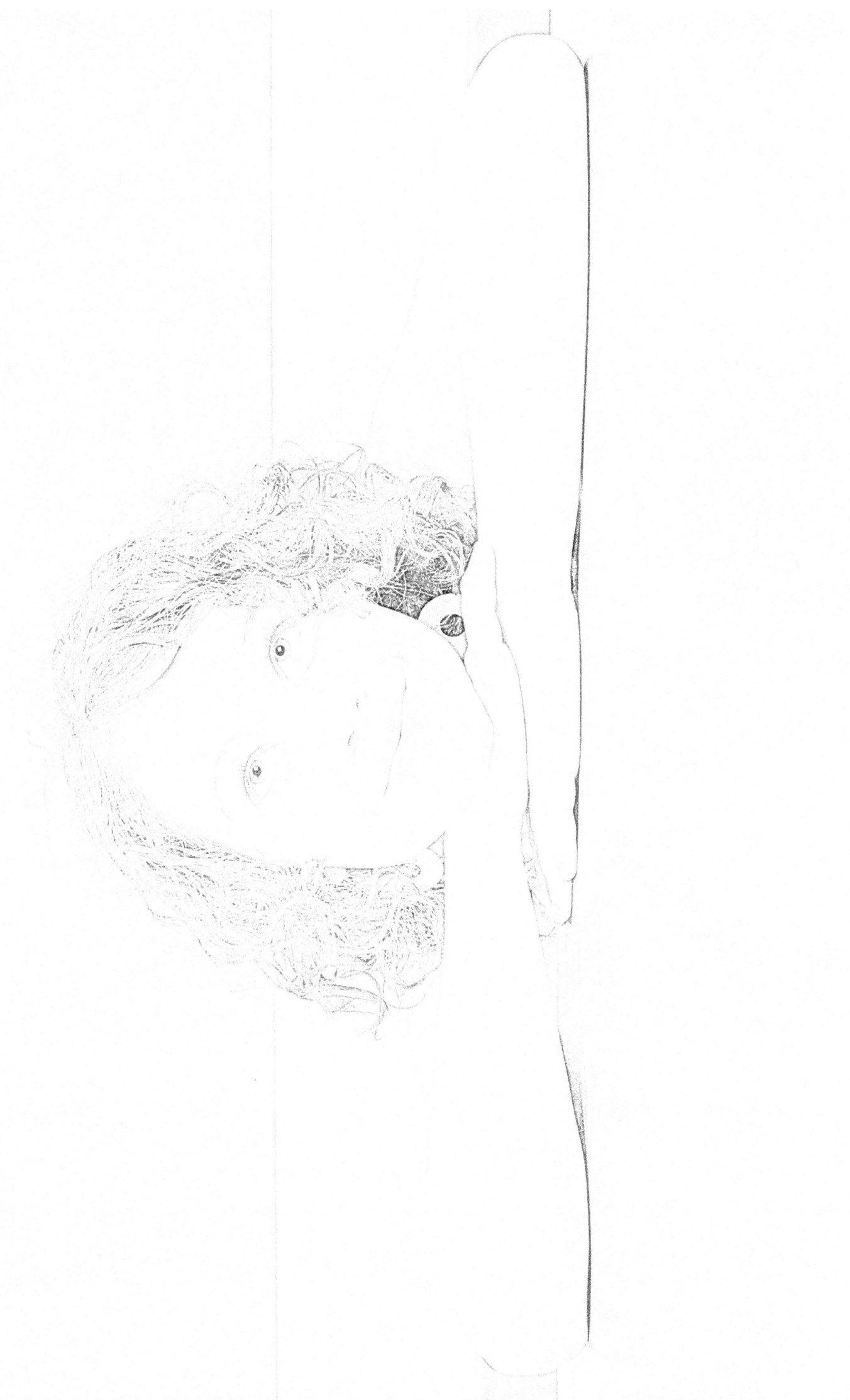

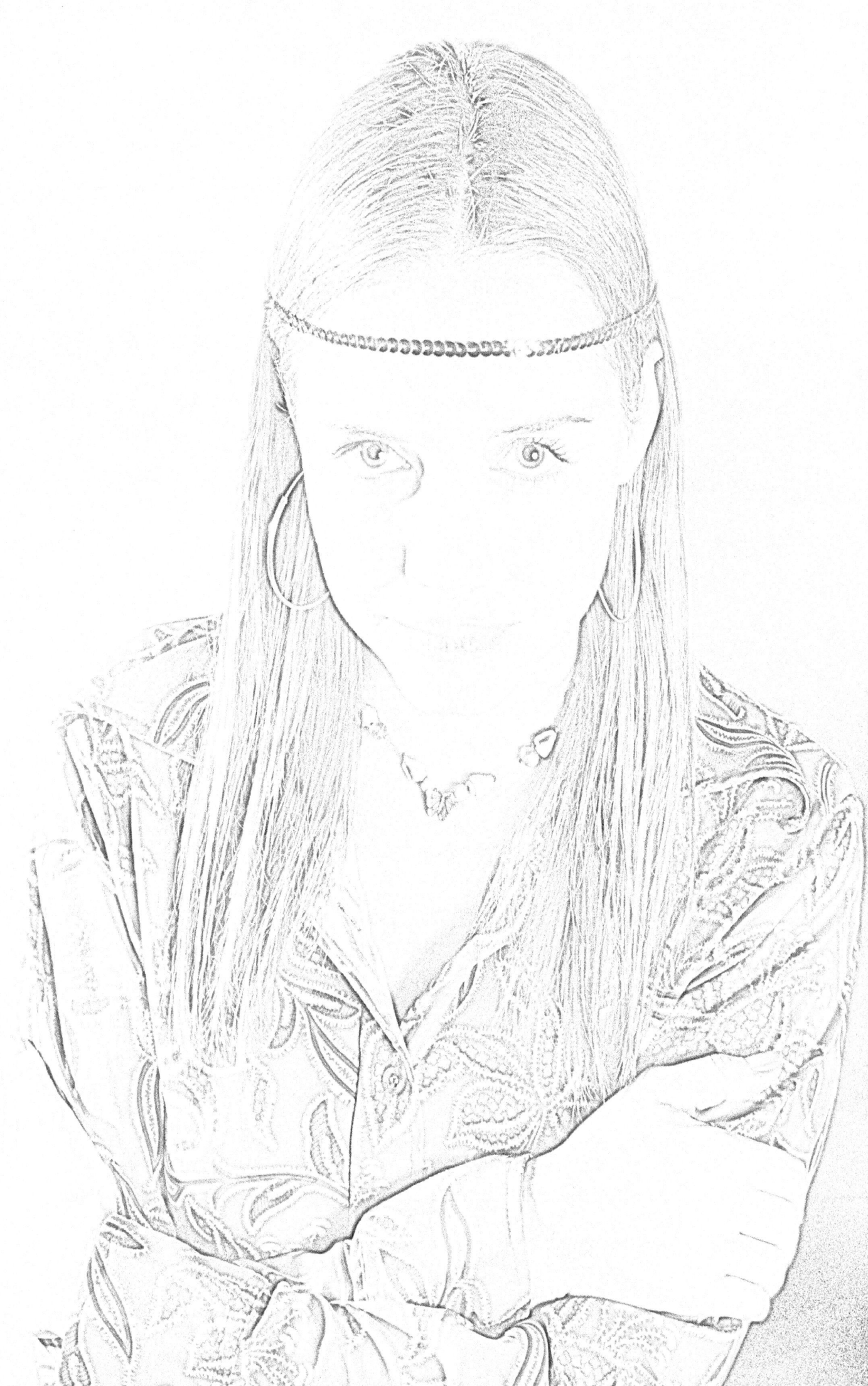

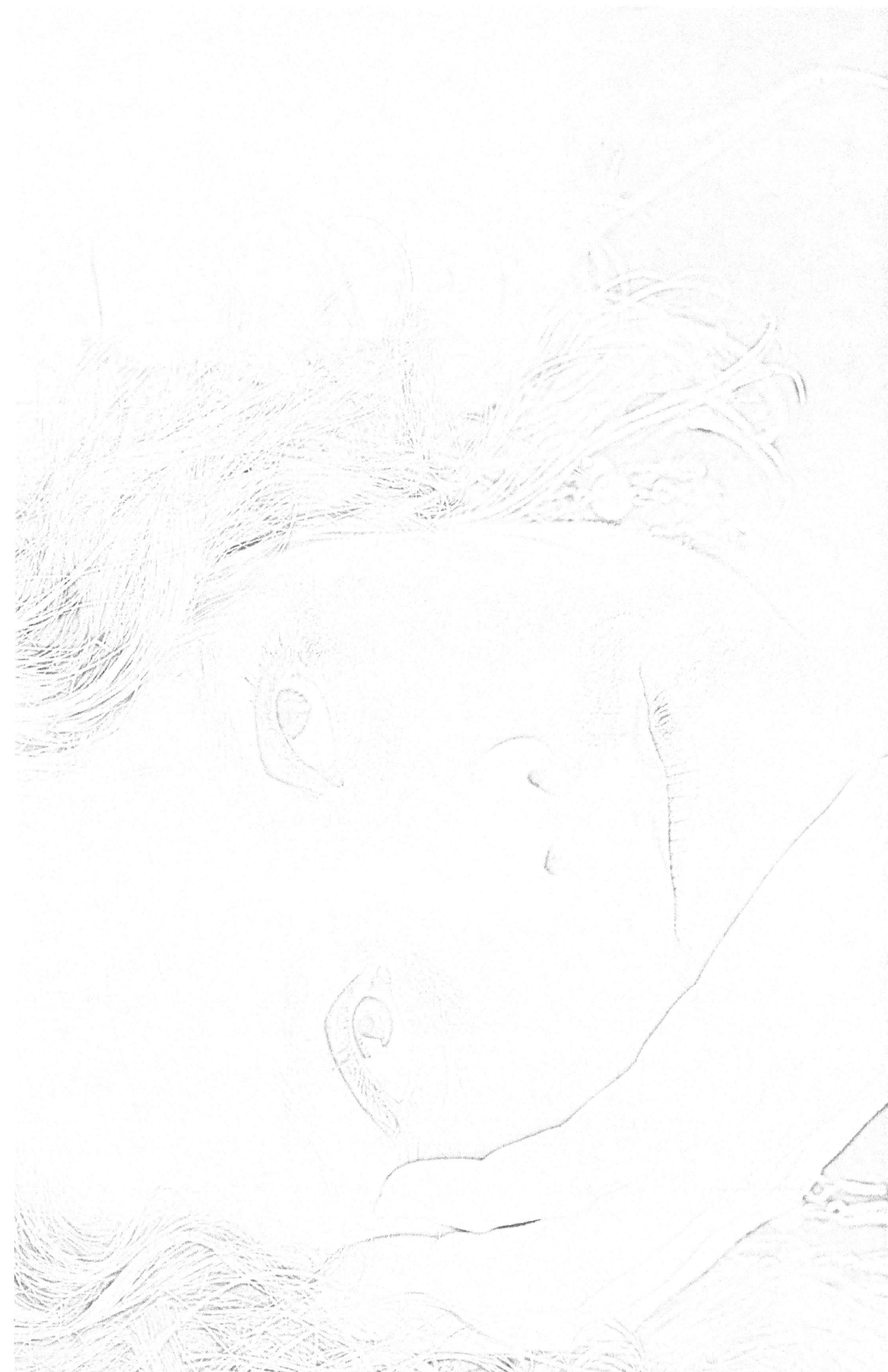

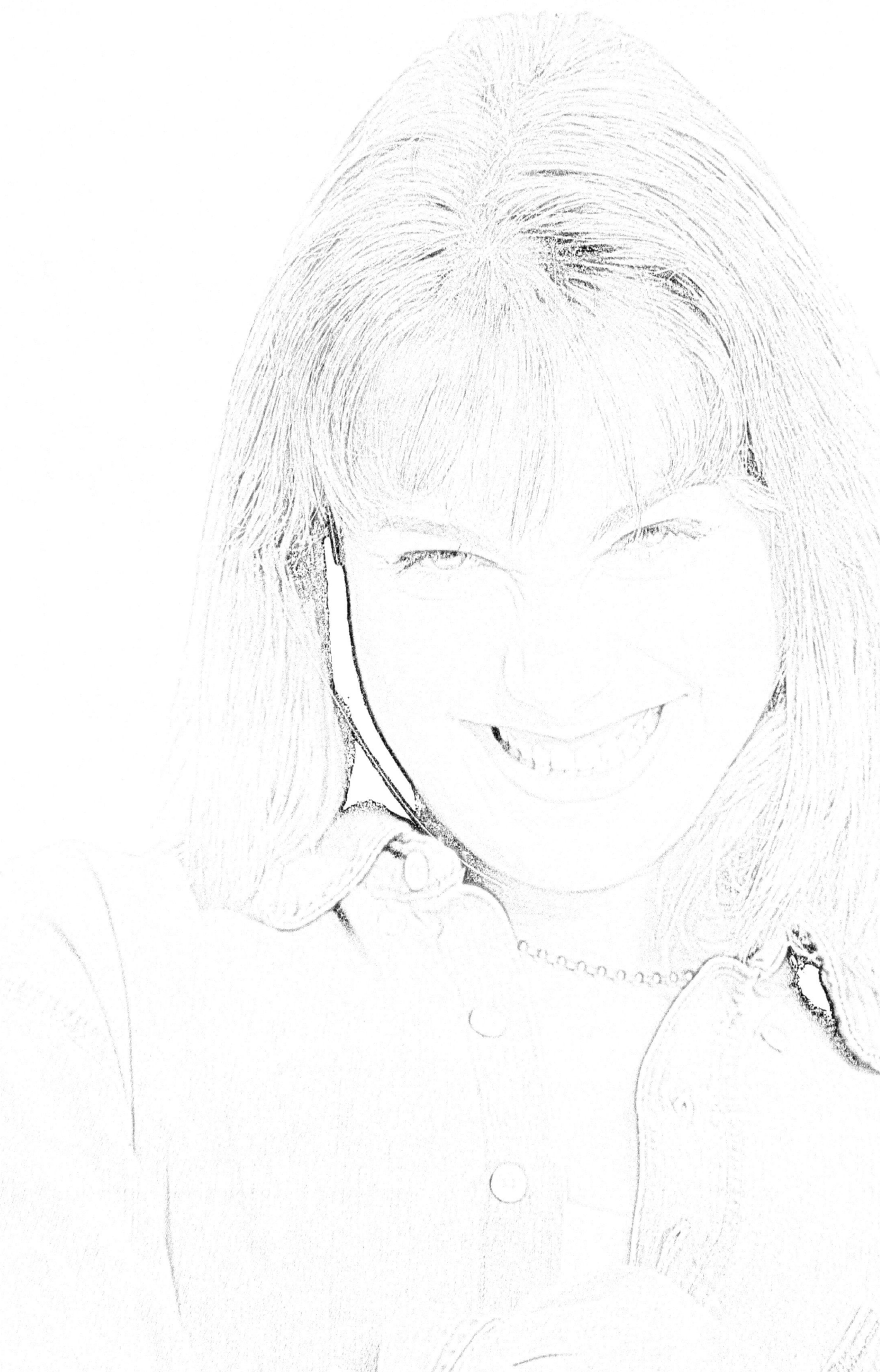

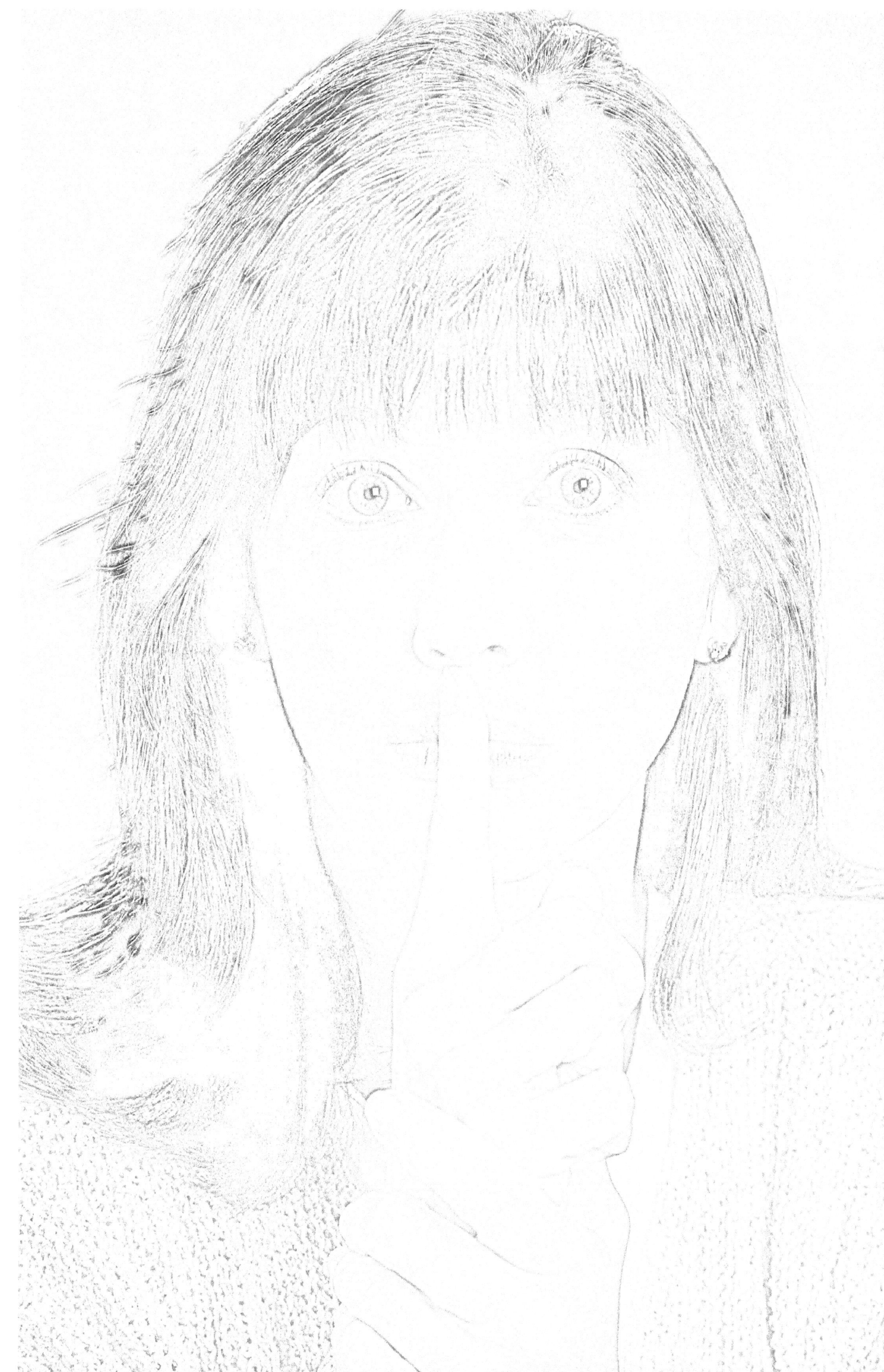

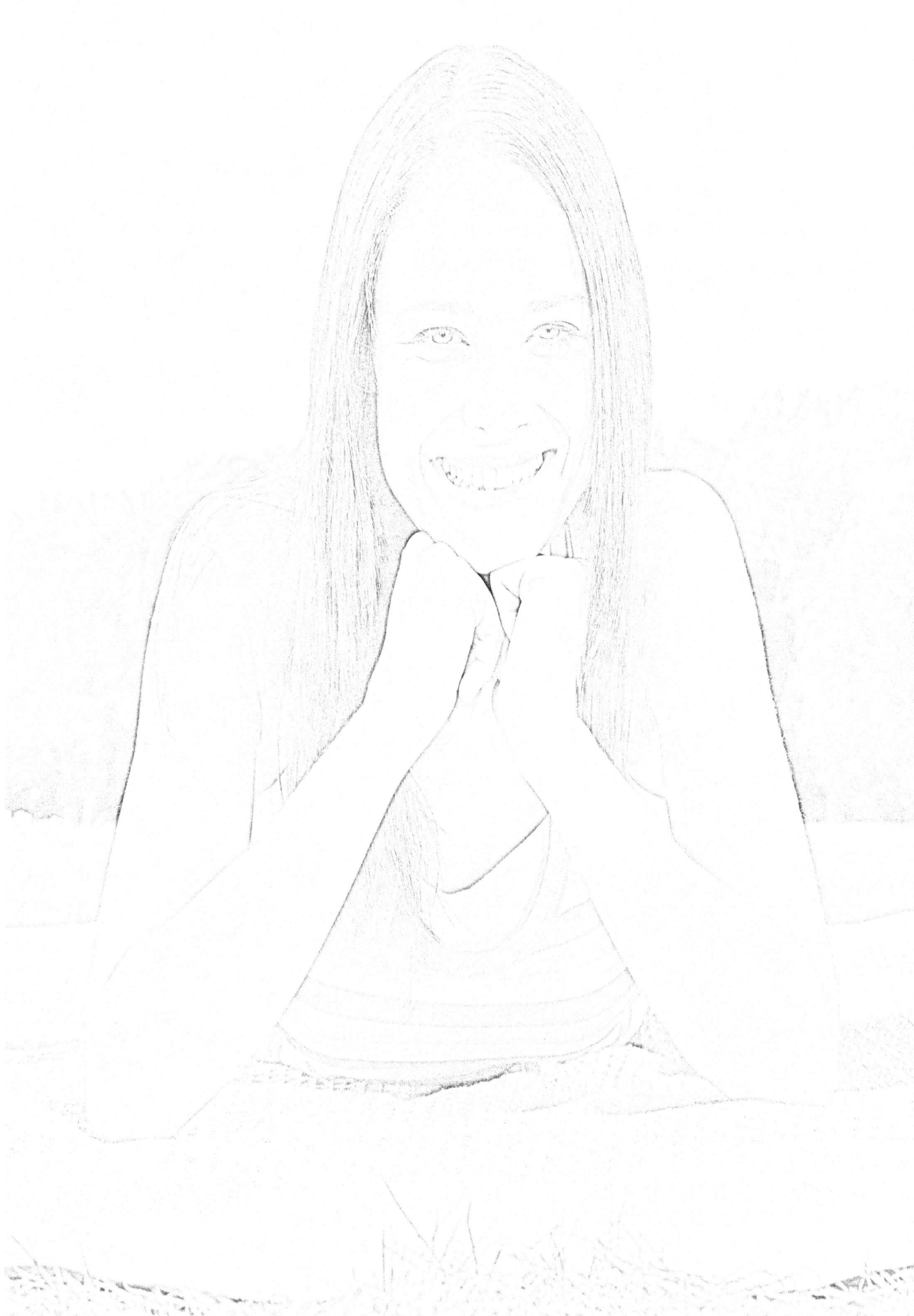

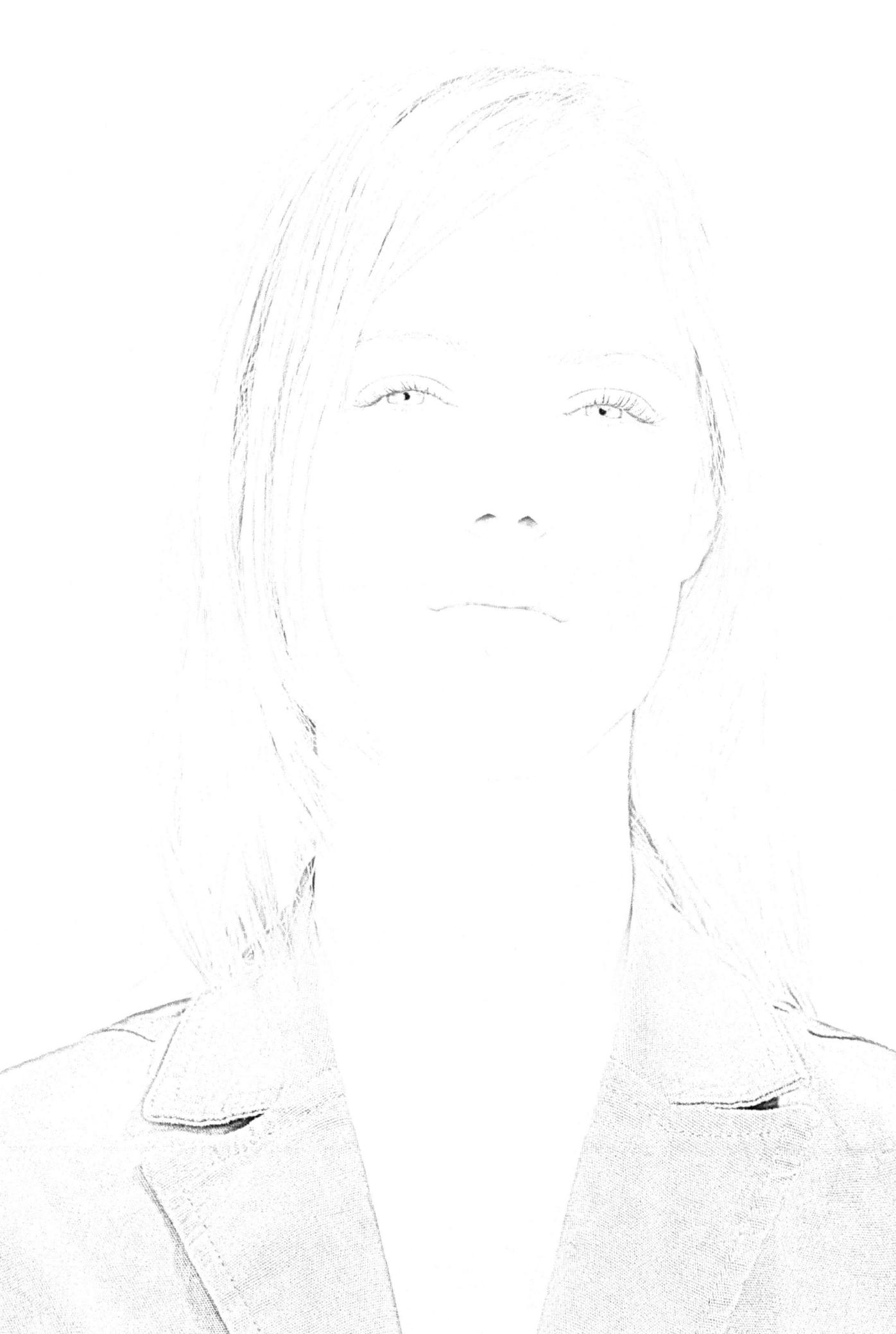

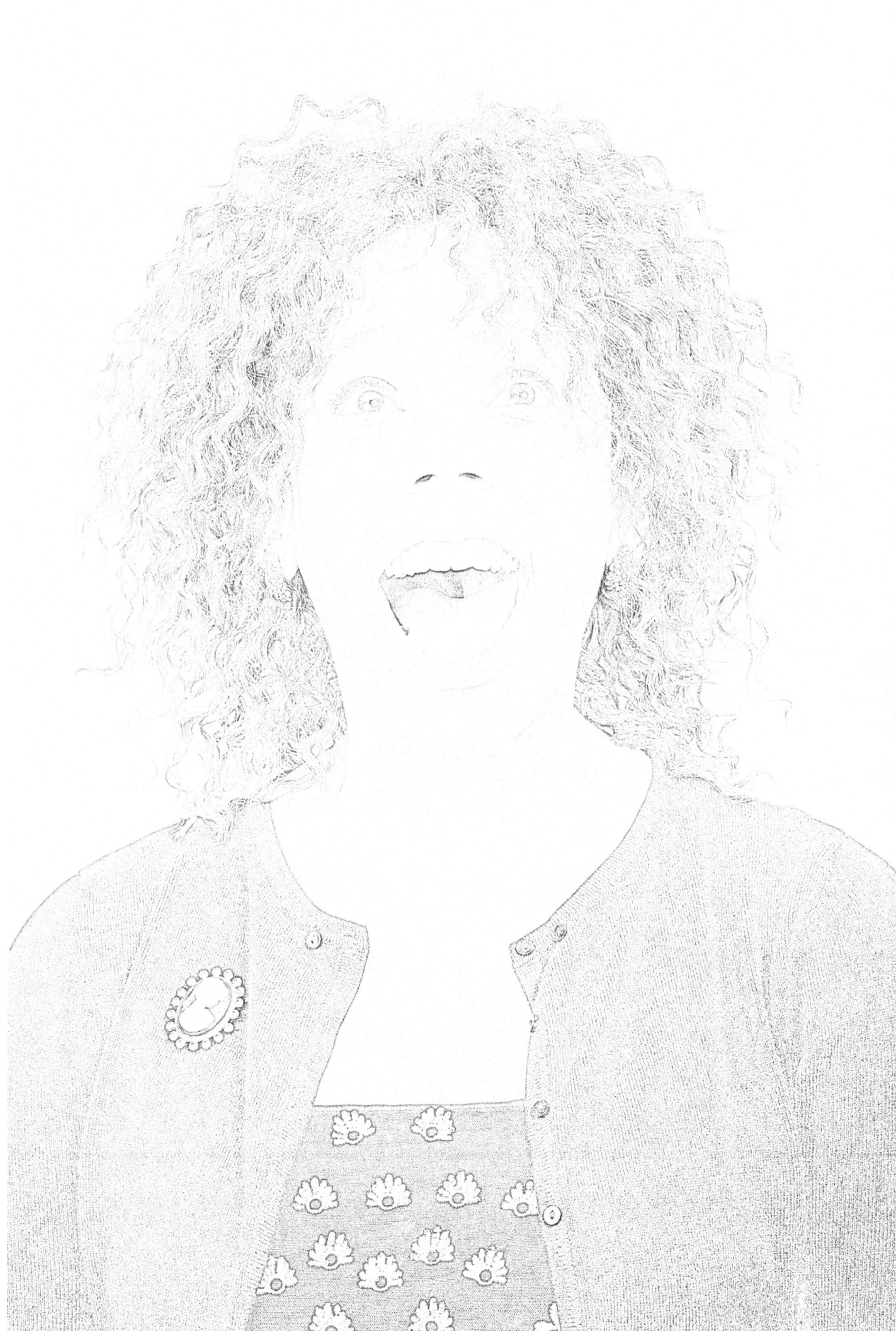

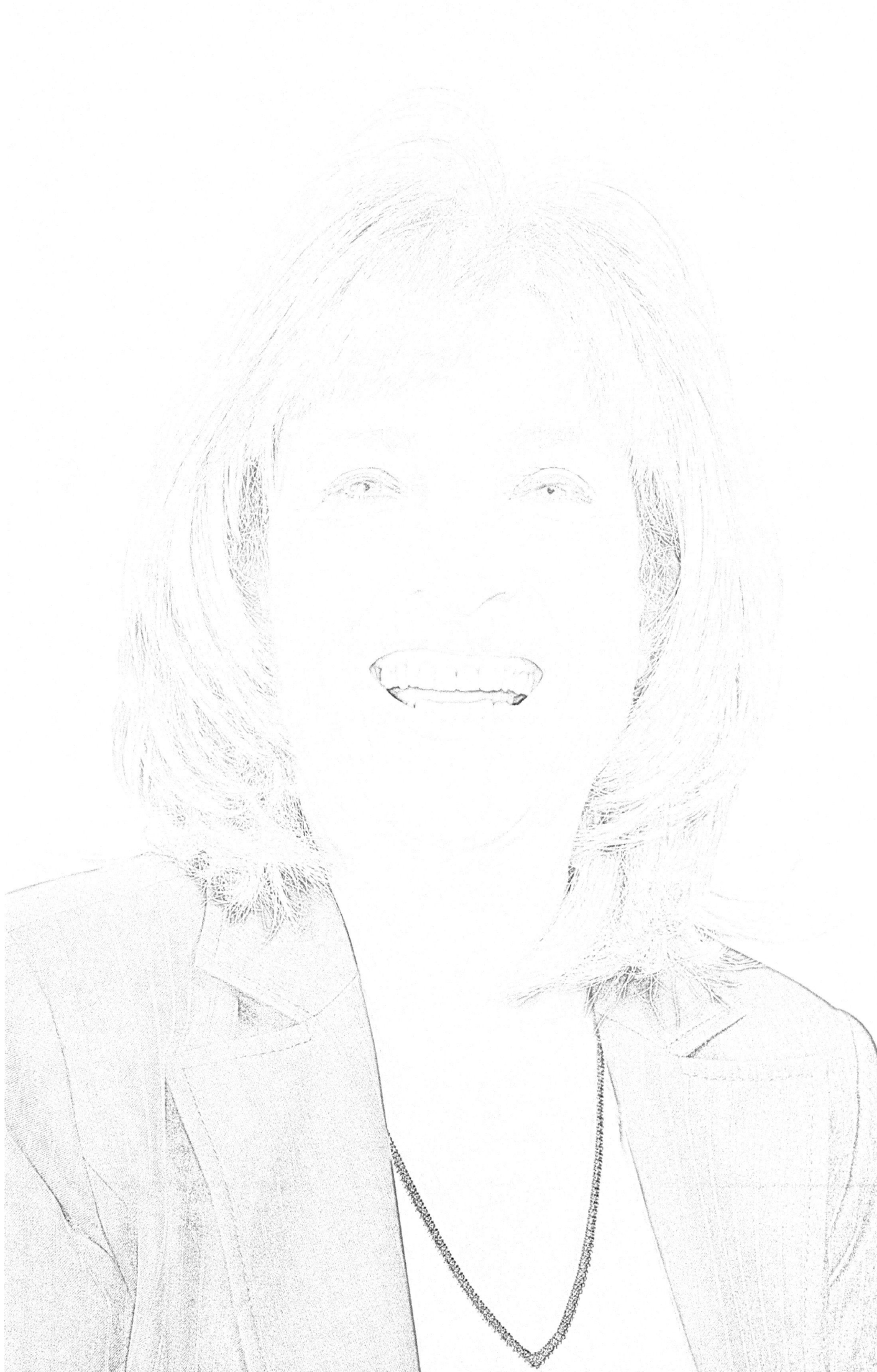

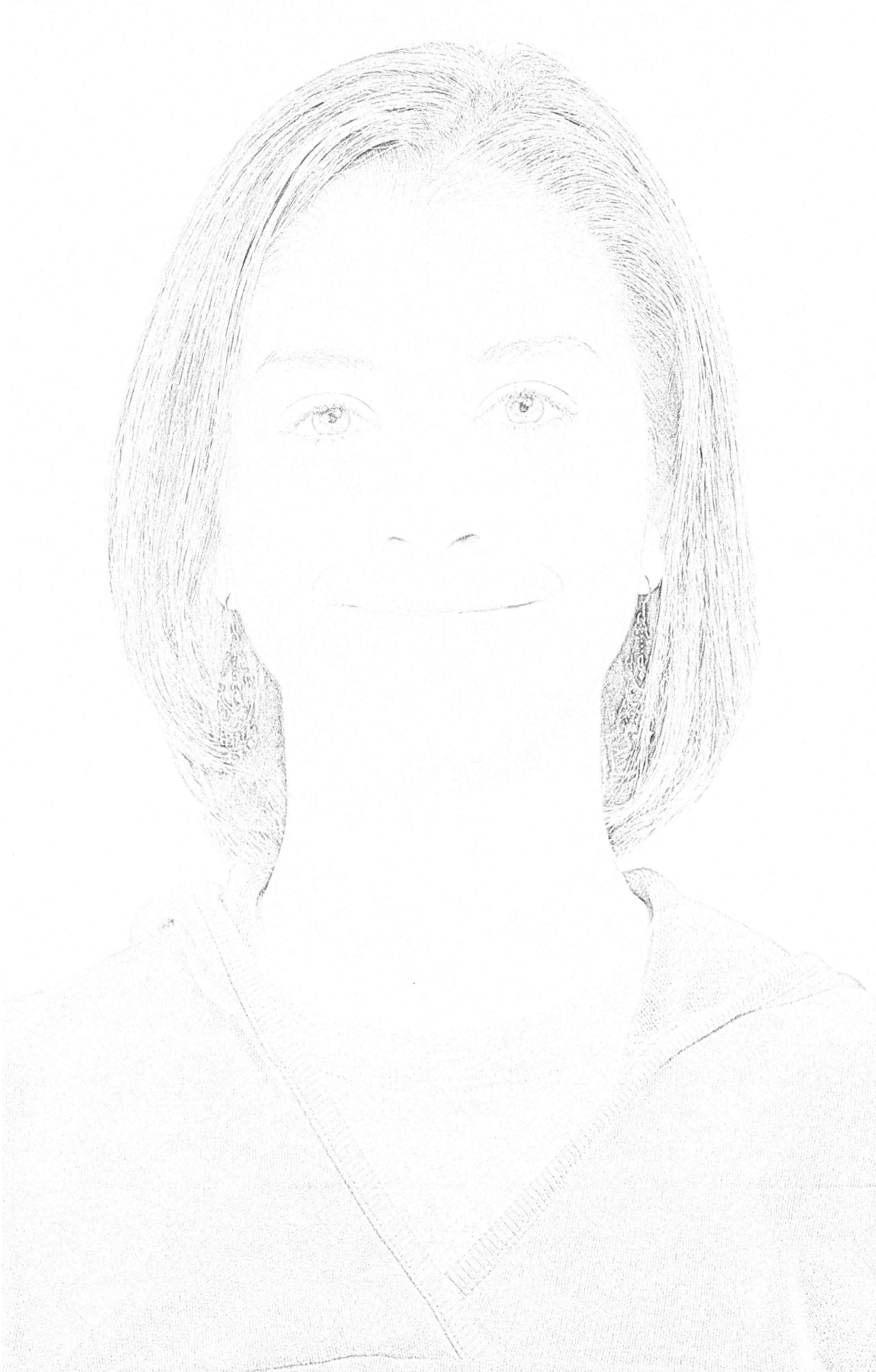

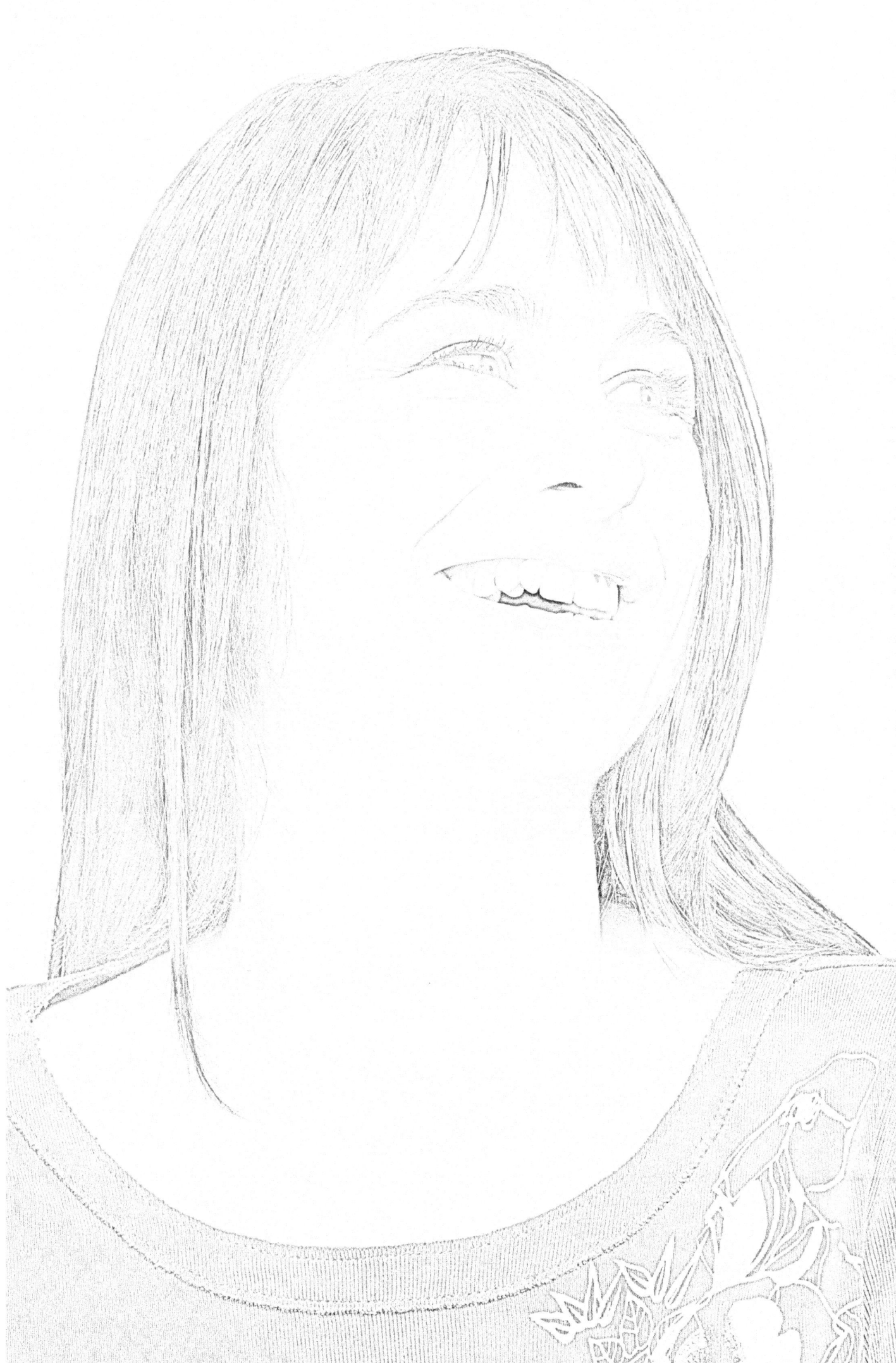

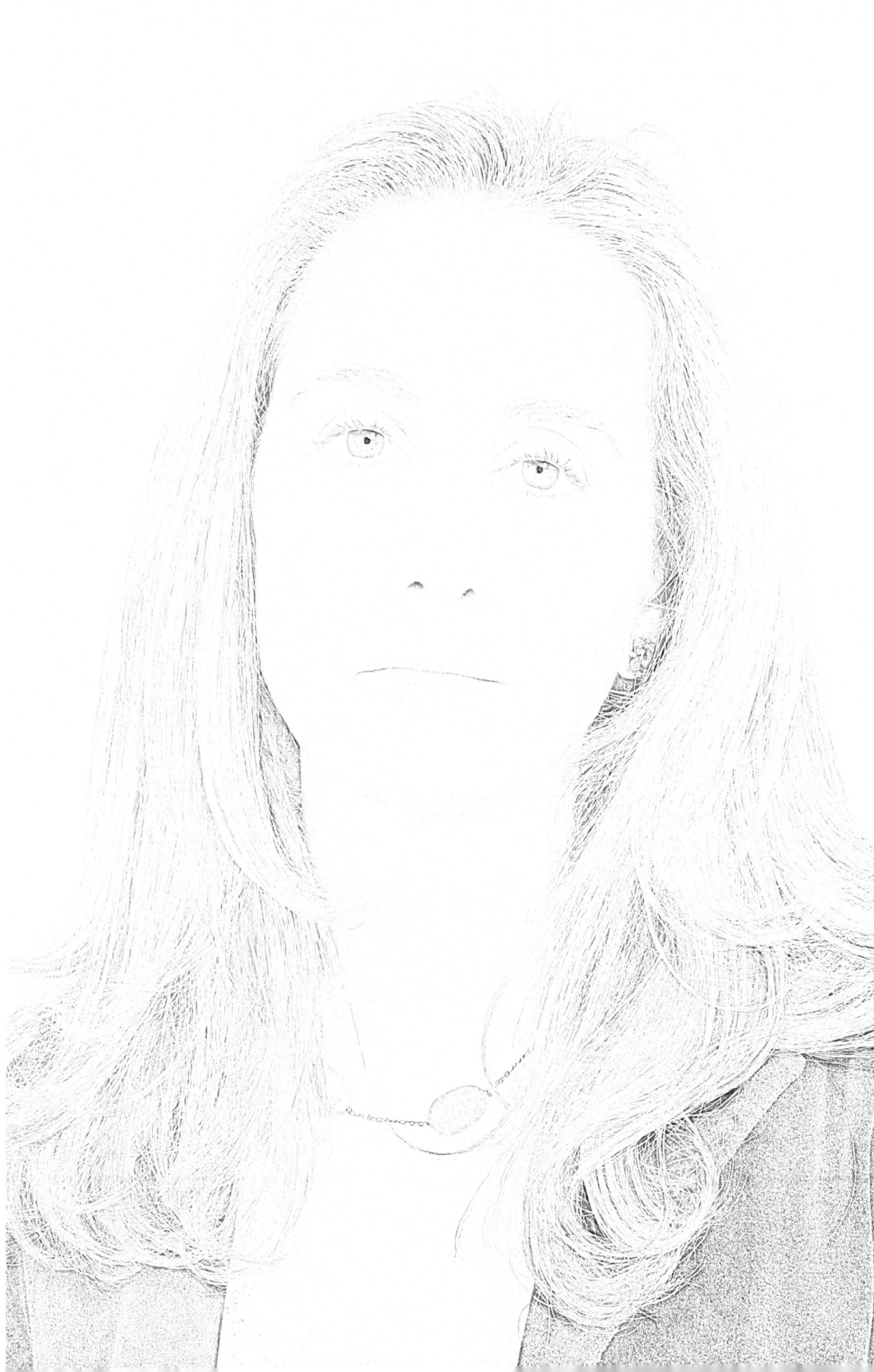

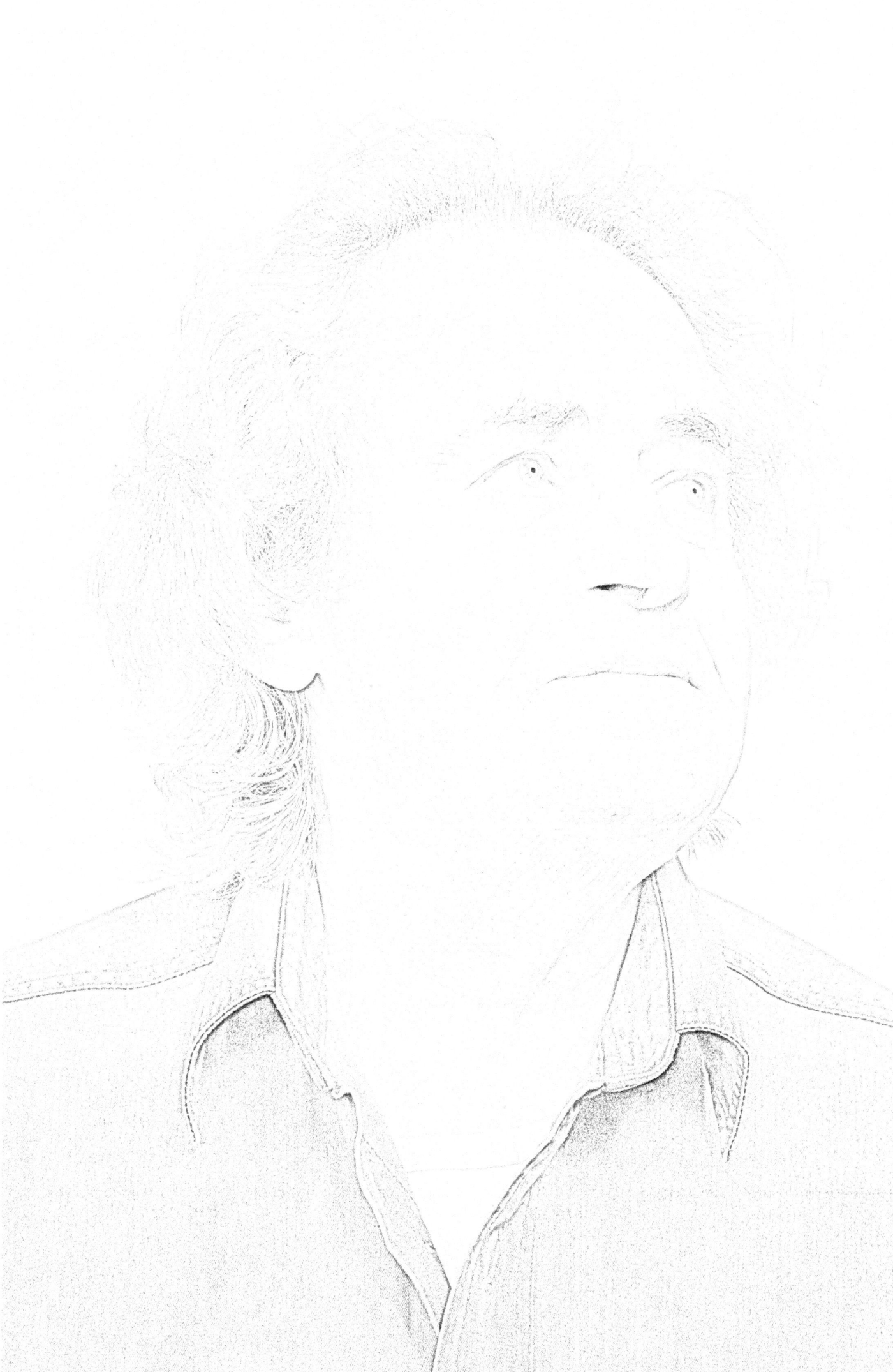

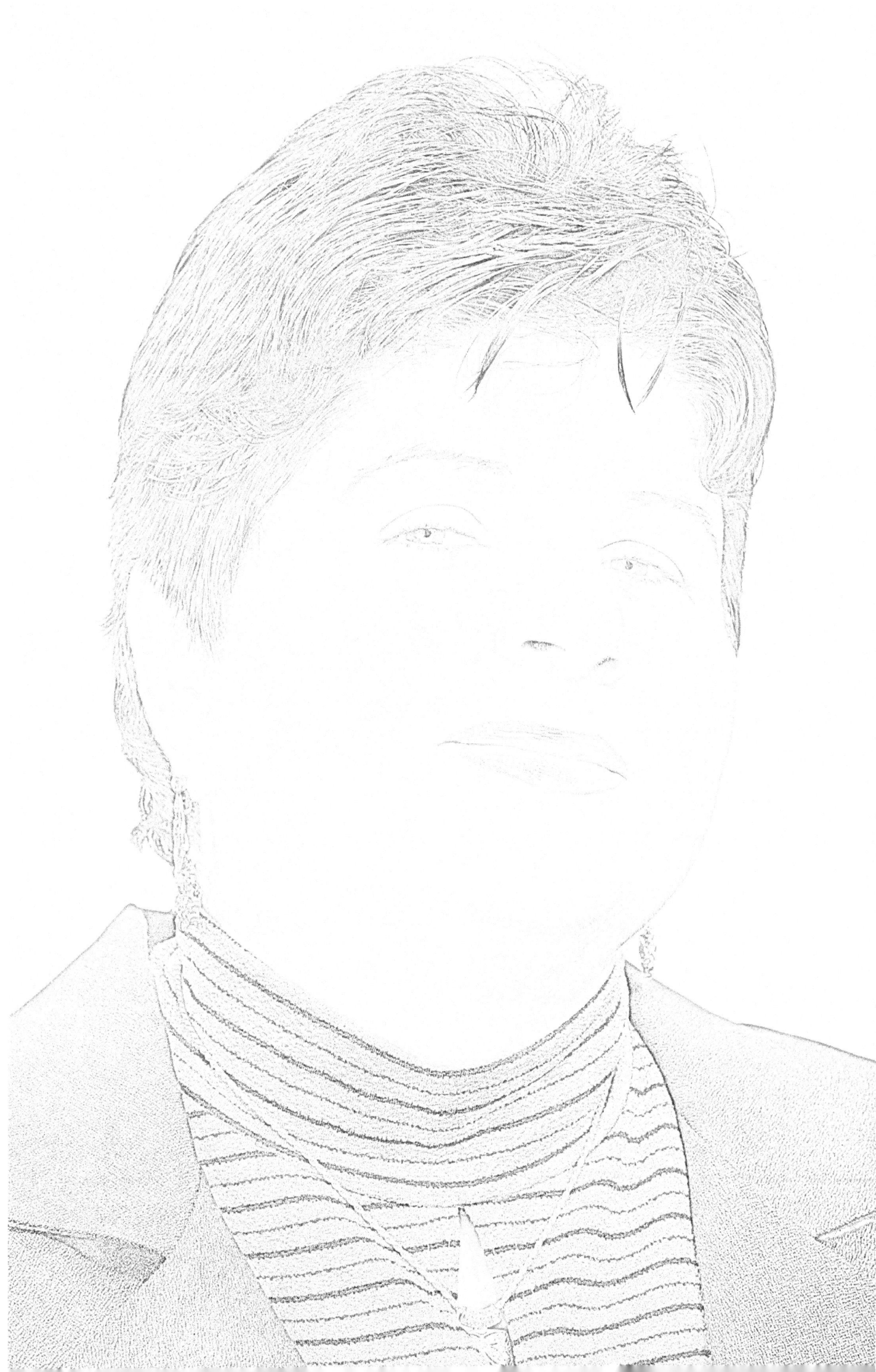

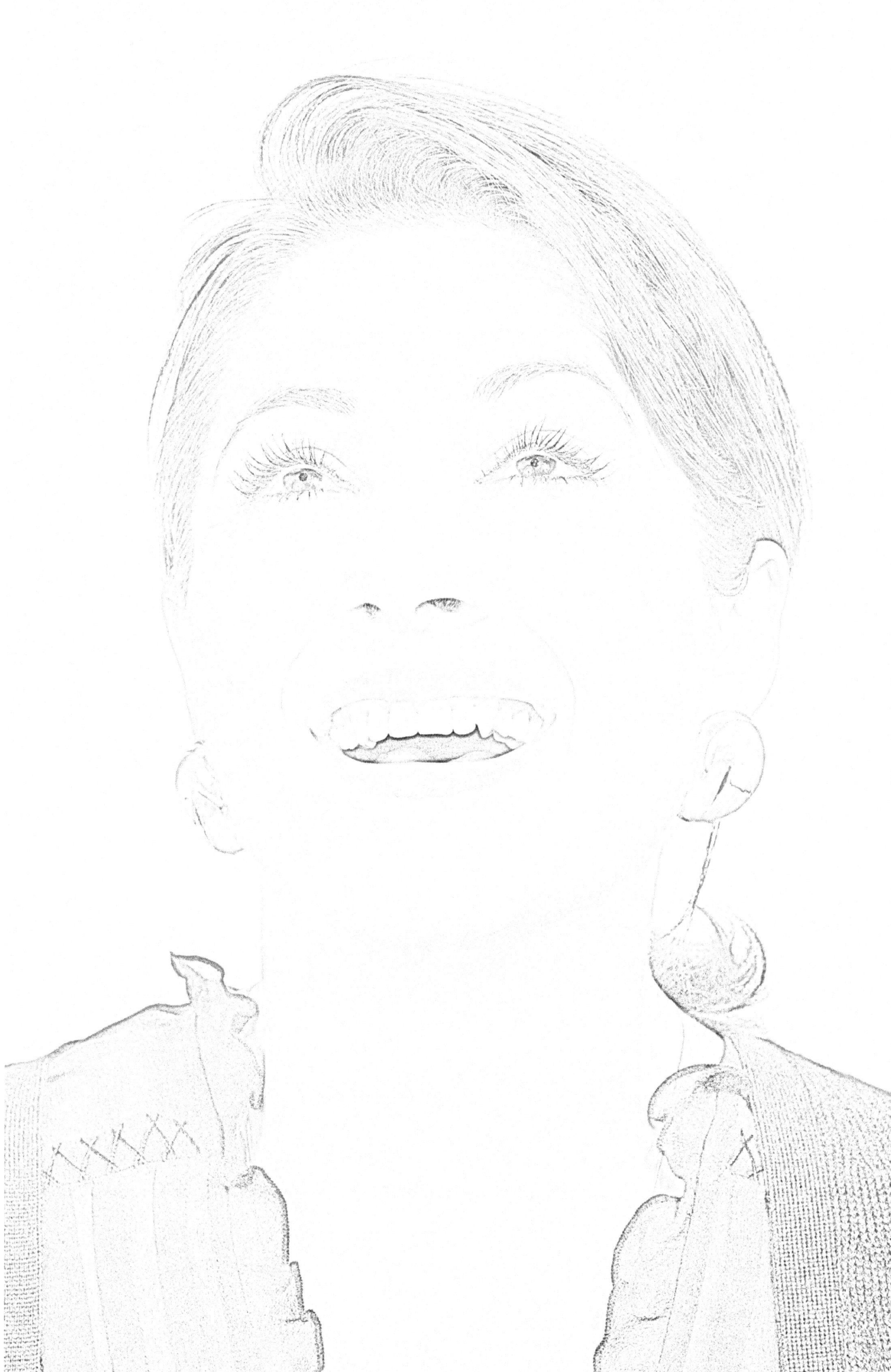

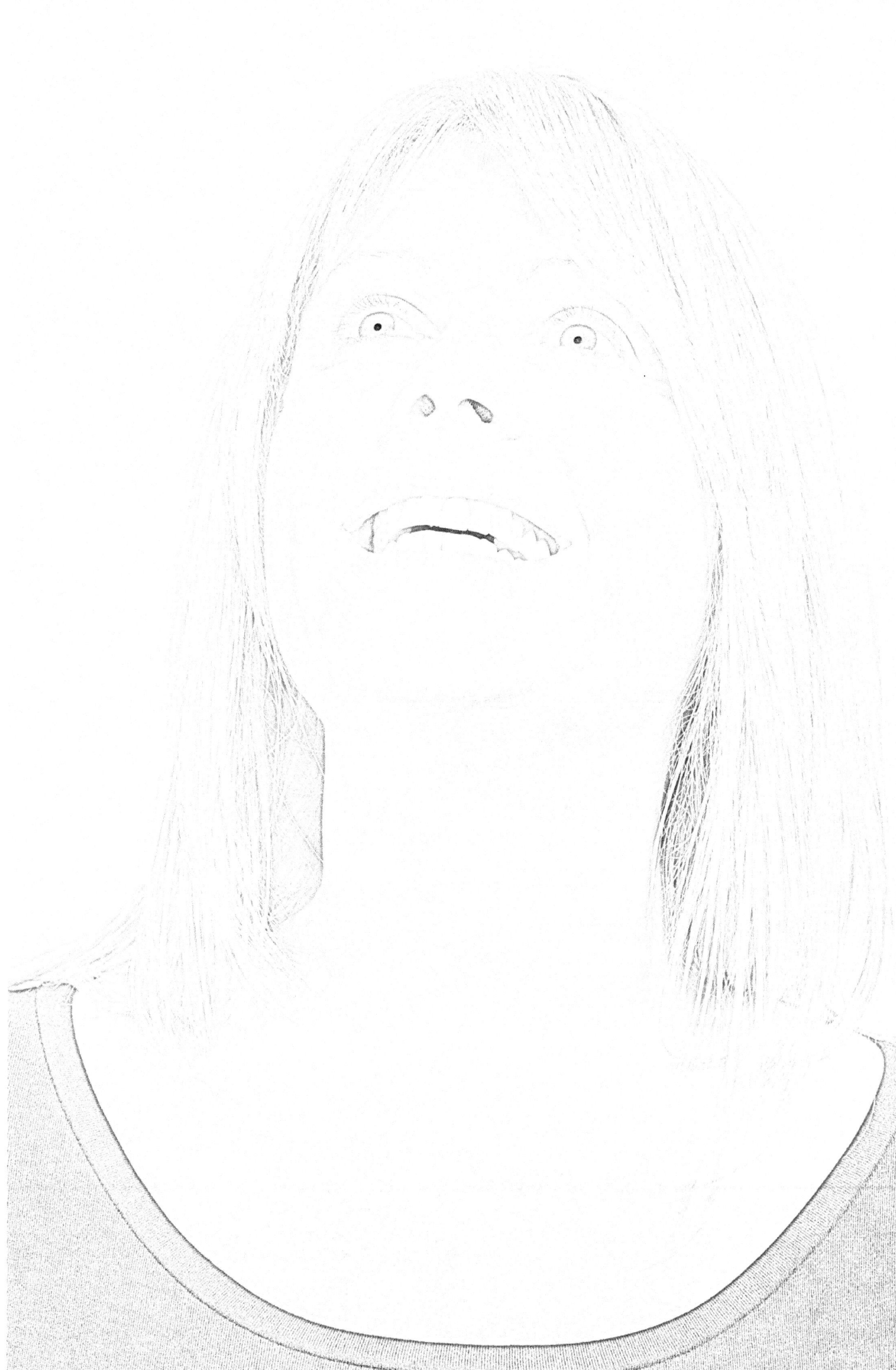

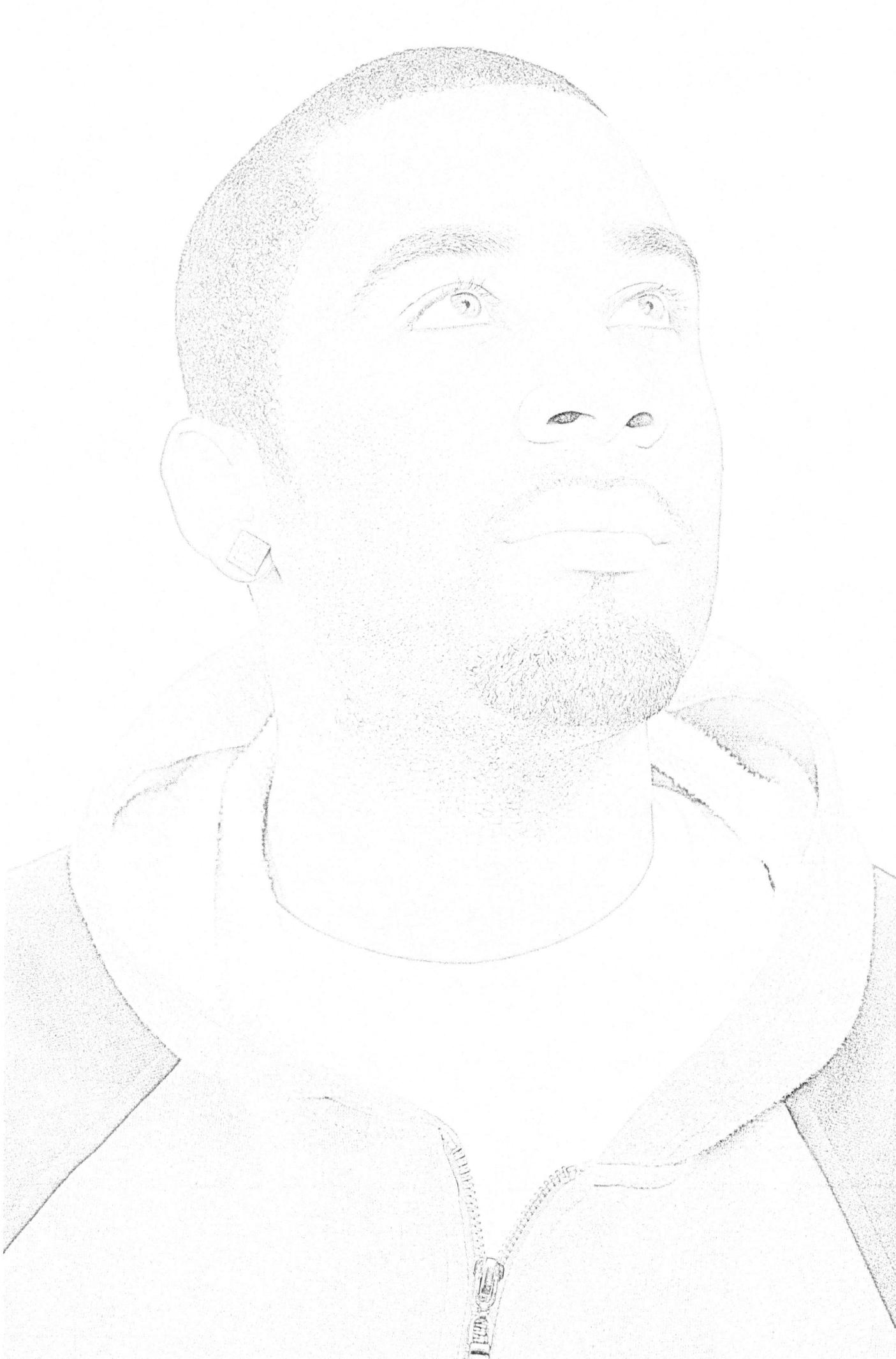

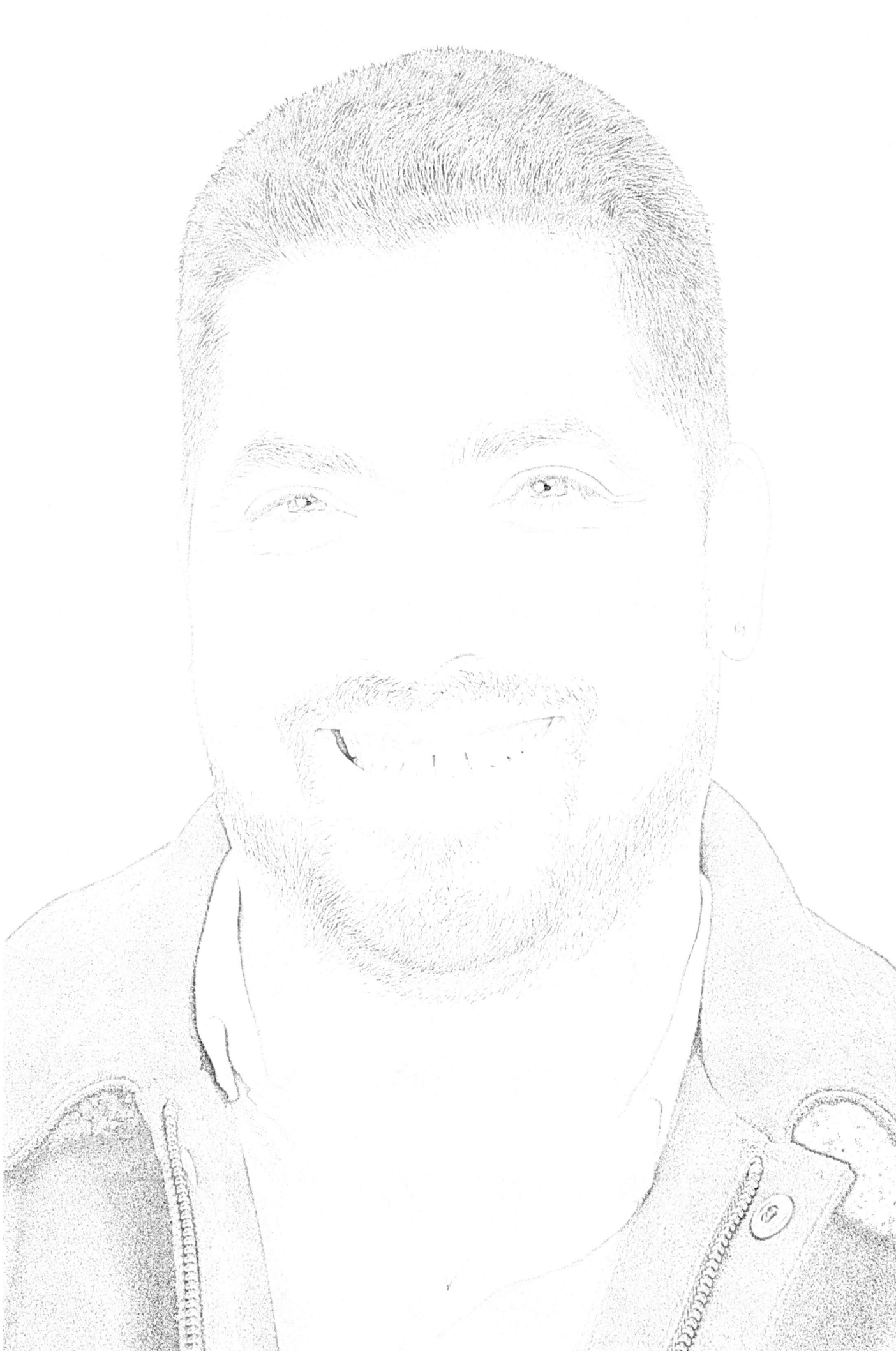

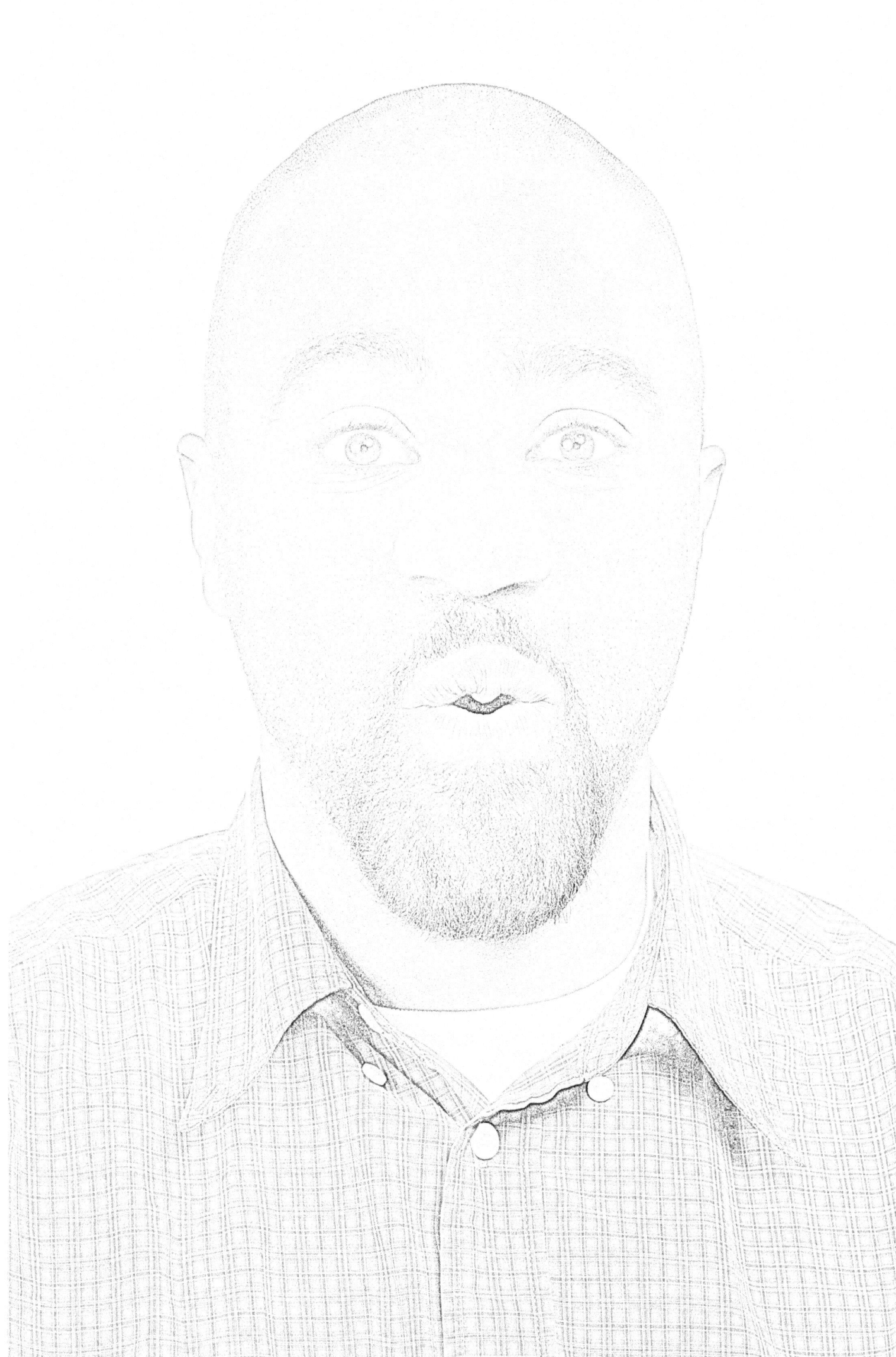

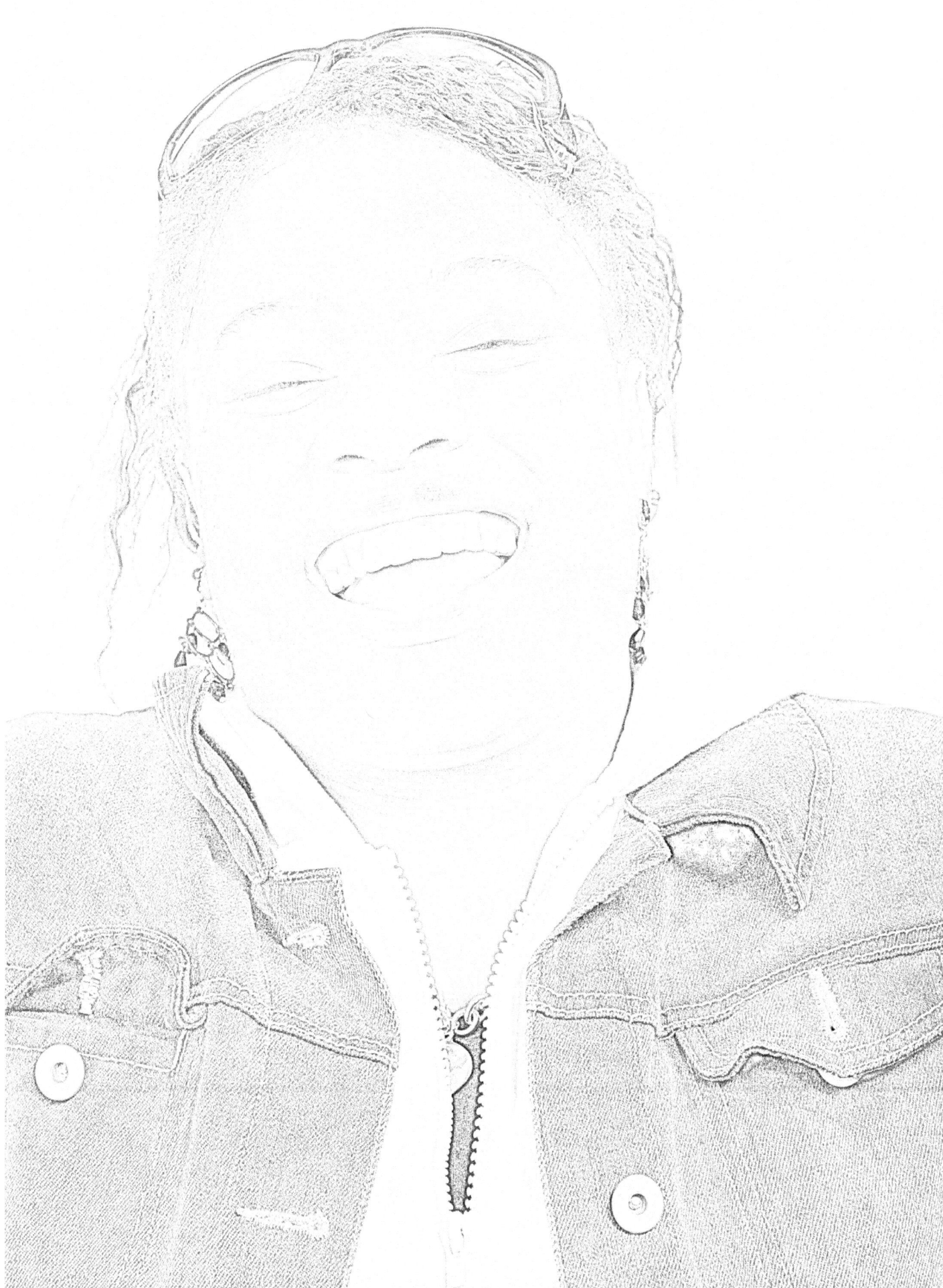

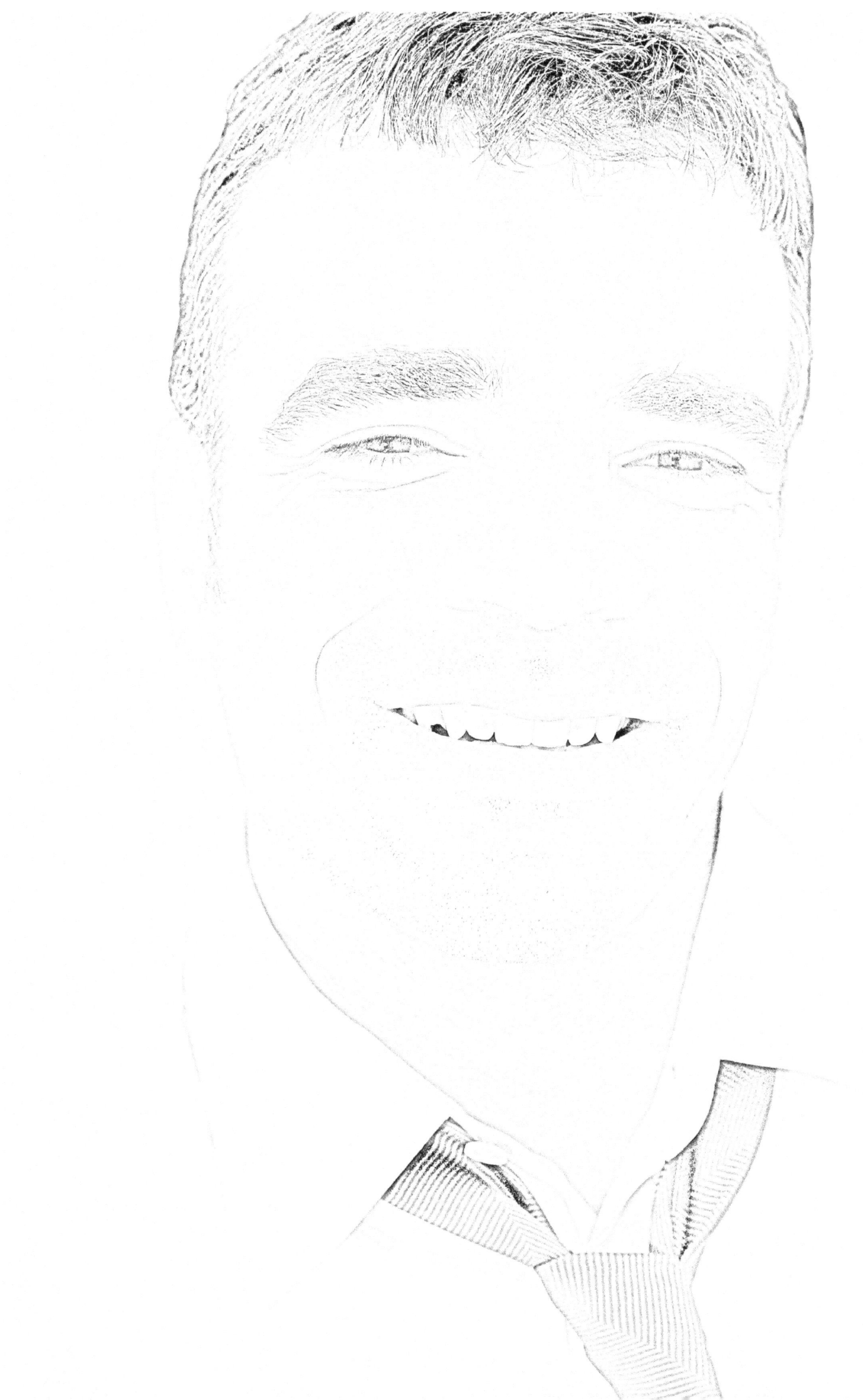